Comp
of
Dawyk Ashton.

Poems From My Heart

Darryl Ashton

Copyright © 2017 Darryl Ashton

All rights reserved.

ISBN-13978-1542626842
ISBN-10: 1542626846

Acknowledgements: Special thanks go to Kieran Chapman of Bumble Print, Durham, UK, who has put this book together. Without his valuable help – this book wouldn't be possible. All the poems in this book are the copyright of Darryl Ashton. No unauthorised copying of any items in this book is permitted without permission from the author.

About the Author...Darryl Ashton:

Darryl Ashton is now medically retired, but he was a silver service Restaurant Manager where his skills took him to land a job on the QE2. He is single, and has no children - well, none that he knows about!

He is a very keen writer, mainly of poetry, covering all kinds of topics; including, humour and more serious writings too. He thrives on political satire, and is equipped with a fantastic, and very wicked sense of humour matched with an incredible imagination.

Darryl also does stand-up comedy poem performances and is involved with various charity work. At one time, he raised an incredible £50,000 just by reading his own poems. His poems have also won several major competitions and he is also a leading reader of poems at various poetry groups on the Fylde Coast, Blackpool, Cleveleys and Lytham, all in the sunny and very friendly borough of Lancashire.

Darryl is originally from Great Harwood, a little town on the border with Accrington and Blackburn. He is a keen teller of jokes, and writing just about anything that takes his interest. Darryl says he's a late starter - he has been writing his poetry for only five years! And he's only just got to grips with his computer.

One really surprising thing that happened to Darryl was receiving an invitation from Her Majesty the Queen, to go to Buckingham Palace to actually meet the Queen where she complimented him on his poems and his fundraising efforts. Darryl also won first prize in a world-wide Elvis Presley poem competition which was organised by

Graceland - Darryl was invited to Graceland where he performed his prize-winning poems featuring Elvis Presley. Darryl is also due to appear on Britain's Got Talent this year as a stand up comedian and a comedy poet.

This is Darryl's second book of poems - which includes a vast selection of his own poems. From political satire, comedy, spiritual, gospel, romance and all other kinds of poems. There's even a grand selection of comedy scripts featuring Abbott and Costello, Fawlty Towers...The Return! There really is something for everyone in this fascinating book of poems. It is a must-have book for anyone who loves poetry. Please be warned: Once you pick this book up and start to read it - you won't want to put it down again!!!!

A CHRISTMAS TALE...DRESS REHEARSAL

Christmas is coming
Everyone's getting stressed,
The Infant Christmas Production
Is putting us to the test.

We're on the way to Bethlehem,
The children are finally dressed,
The costumes have seen betters days —
It's a pity they weren't pressed!

Joseph is teasing the donkey
Who is terribly, terribly slow
And has now stopped altogether
Because he doesn't want to go.

We've got too many angels,
The stars are thick on the ground,
Yet when we ask them all to sing
It's hard to hear a sound.

The Kings forgot the presents,
The camels haven't appeared,
Mary is looking tearful
Just as we all had feared.

Instead of 'Sorry, there is no room'
The innkeeper opens the door,

He tells them they can go inside
And sit down on the floor.

The villagers are fighting,
The shepherds kick the sheep,
Some of the narrators
Are sounding half asleep.

The doll was in the manger
Now Mary takes it out,
She's gone from tearful to excited
And she's waving it about.

Then comes the Grand Finale,
There's a puddle on the floor,
It's time to call a finish
Or there'll be a whole lot more.

So things are just as always
Becoming extremely fraught –
But the parents will think it's brilliant,
That's such a comforting thought!

                The Panto was a success,
that
we do now know,
All those girls and boys – they really did all glow.
Merry Christmas to all the children, as they all do play,
But don't forget to go to bed early – as Santa arrives on his sleigh!

A drunken Santa has made it through,
And beat the traffic queue!
He now flies home to Lapland,
With a sherry in his hand!

He shouts; "Merry Christmas, folks, and gives a cheeky wink",
He flies away, oh so fast – he daren't even blink!

A CHRISTMAS BIRTH

A new heart for Christmas –
is one for sale?
If I find one – I will so hail.
To find true love is a mission
of mine,
To meet my princess – and
feel divine.

Oh come oh ye loved one –
and pledge your love –
I feel it now – our own love
trove.
For my heart beats fast – as
fast as a bullet,
For the sake of top gun – I
yearn to love it.

A newly born life – is a gift
from the lord,
Welcome my friends –
please, come aboard.
Thou shall see my true love
spurn,
As my soul in torment – will
now learn.

May the spirit of the gods
be mightier now,
As where my love is – I will
find somehow.
The Christmas spirit I fail to
feel,
Have I sinned – I beg to kneel?

The holy mask – is open to all –
A mask of disguise – it must enthrall.
To see the future is a sight to be told;
'I see in your spirit – a sight to behold.'

The baby Jesus is born to hail,
A new beginning – I hear you all wail.
His timing is fine – and at this time –
That's why I love – to write my rhyme.

Mother, Mary, the virgin mother,
Hugs her baby up to her shoulder.
Joseph too, looks up at the stars –
As God looks down – and ends all wars.

The birth of Jesus – is almost here,
But some of us do - shed a tear.
May the heart of love, be given as a gift –
As the power of love – shall end all rift.

My heart, my love, is what
I do yearn,
My heart and my soul, does
slowly churn.
Behold, my love – I'll see
thee at mass –
So I'll finally say; 'A Happy
Christmas.

Always have hope – and
faith be known,
Then mankind, will soon be
reborn.
May the love of life, be
blessed to you –
And a Happy New Year –
will now come true.

A BROKEN HEART

When you have a broken
heart, nothing else matters,
You feel all alone – and your
life just stops – you feel in
total tatters.

Your heart just breaks – as
you slowly die,
That is how you feel – you
cannot deny.

The prospect of losing your
true love, doesn't seem real,
But you must try and mend
your ways – as you feel a total
betrayal.

Just hang in there as best you
can – that is good advice,
Then one day in the future –
everything will be nice.

It may take time – there's no
doubt, but it will all work out fine,
And you, and your darling – will
again feel so sublime!

A little angelic miracle, that is
what will happen,
The angels will mend your
broken heart – and love will
surely sharpen.

So, fear not, that broken heart,
as everything will be ace,
As you, and your mended heart –
sing a song to love and grace.

A CARER'S STORY

In each square mile, so many sit
Alone, In need of care,
To bathe, to eat, to take their meds,
To dress, or wash their hair.

Day by day, the TV on,
Old dramas blaring out,
A threadbare chair, the pressure foam,
A bed with pads laid out.

Drinks lined up between the calls,
A 'lifeline' round the neck,
Everything is left to hand,
As no more can they trek.

'I'm sick of this', they often moan,
'It's no fun getting old.
'Embarrassing, you doing this',
Caregivers often are told.

It's not a life they're living now,
They've no choice but exist,
Basic needs are done for them,
A client on a list.

And while some family do pop round,
Ten minutes here and there,
The burden borne is never told,
But speaks volumes in the air.

Gardens overgrown with weeds,
A gate with broken hinge,
Paint flaking from the windowsills,
It makes the neighbours cringe.

Stories abound in childhood games,
'The wicked witch lives there',
'Don't go near the dirty house',
As kids, they try to scare.

In one square mile commuters rush,
They see a rundown house,
But never give a second thought
As on with life they push.

A tell-tale sign to those who know,
A key-box on the wall.
A secret code to let us in,
To check on one and all.

In each square mile so many sit,
And behind the walls they hide,
Watching life, but never seen,
Until the day they died.

We are real people – that is true,
All we want is to be friends with you.
It isn't our fault we've got old,
But our long hard story – it must be told.

God bless our carers, that we all say,
I wish you all a terrific new day.
We welcome you as our friend,
To care for us – is your trend.

The carers we know, all work so hard,
But sometimes they smoke in the yard!
We have no problems with them smoking a cig,
Only the government condemn them so quick – as we ourselves, don't give a fig!
On behalf of my friends – I say to you,
Thank you all – we mean that true.

You are our carers – and we value you,
You really are - a fabulous crew.

THE ANGELIC HEAVENLY CHOIR

The star shines down from
a far
It shines so bright, it glows
on the choir.
The choir of angels – which
sounds so good,
Conducted by the lord, as
we know it should.

The angels are playing their
heavenly sound,
That's why I am heaven
bound?
To hear the music of the
angel choir,
While I sit down within my
chair.

The angels are playing their
instruments so good,
Even the elves are in a good
mood!
Soon they are dancing, as
so is Santa,
This is so true – it isn't my
bantor?

The heaven now rocks, as
the party does swing,
Then good God himself - gets
set to sing?
The whole place is bopping –
and someone does wink,
One elf says to an angel; "

can I buy you a drink?"

So Happy Christmas to you, I mean that so true,
The heavenly music – plays, just for you.
Hear the sound within your dreams,
Enjoy your Christmas – it is magic, it seems!

THE ANGELIC ISLAND OF PARADISE THE PHILIPPINES.

There is an island far away, rich in beauty,
and in love.
The love is evident as you look, all around
you, love is the trove.

The Philippines is a land of beauty, surfing
and fishing is their way?
You'll get a welcome fit for a king, you'll be
their star – while you stay.

Paradise, found, that is true, a land of magic –
just for you?
Just come on in and love will follow, and the
people's love, will all be true?

You'll fly by jet as fast as sound, to the Philippines
you are bound?
As you fly on the jet so pure, the crew are there,
and all so sound.

They say: "thank you, for flying with them.
But, boy, what a pleasure, what a dream"?
You've now reached the island of love, you
are welcomed by the sweet friendly charm.
The charm and the beauty of the Philippines,
a welcome you get – is so warm.

Flowers are dancing to you in delight, asking
you if you've had a good flight?
Yes, you say to the colourful sight, the beauty
is there – and you love the night?

The nightlife is grand – and the people make merry,

As you take the tour on the midnight ferry?
The ferry to whisk you on a tour so charming,
Never before have you felt so amazing?

You sing to the fish and the birds
of the night, the chorus does sound
a sheer delight?
The tour on the ferry has been a
dream, now you wake up – and
you see the light?

The light of the sun as it welcomes
the day, saying hello to a brand new
day?
A brand new day in the paradise isle,
the fabulous Philippines, I'd like to
stay!

So God Bless the Philippines, I mean
that so true, the love you share – is
very caring.
I go to your island in my dreams –
as one day, soon, that's where I'll be
living!

The island culture, is so special, the
colour is awesome, boy, we love her?
So welcome, my friends to the island
of dreams, you come with your blessings –
cos you do care.

The passion, the love, the animal world,
all live as one on their friendly earth?
No one does harm them – as love does
rule, the Philippines, we bless you, that
is our birth?

Good bye for now, I end my trip, as I do
hope you enjoyed this angelic island.
Go now, my friends have a safe journey
home, come back soon, the Philippines,
so grand?

THE ANGELIC PHILIPPINES

God smiled down upon
this land –
And took the saviour by
the hand.
He said; 'I want to bless
these loving people –
And build a land with a
holy temple?'

A temple of love – and of
prayer,
When to the lord – they
will all cheer.
A blessing from the almighty
king,
When you and you're loved
one shall wear the ring.

"Come forth. my flock, I ask
you near,
Why do you cry – and shed
a tear?"
The lord almighty has the
blessings to bestow,
Even when you are feeling
so low.
Hold out thy hand – and the
lord shall kiss,
Then you'll be in eternal bliss.

The Philippines are a shrine
of true love,
Given, and blessed, by the
good lord, above.
The charm of his love does
extend to us all,
As we give thanks – and hear
his call.

He blessed the nature and
the animals –
Giving them all life – and lots
of thrills.
The seas and the fish are also
blessed,
The fishermen, too, made a
special request.

Some people are poor – they
struggle to live,
Why can't the lord now forgive?
The land is alive – as the people
survive,
The lord will bless them – and
keep them alive.

The beautiful flowers that grow
so cute,
You can view this sight – as you
pick the fruit.
The blessings of the lord are in
our dreams,
God bless the angelic' Philippines.

THE BEAUTIFUL LOVE OF THE PHILIPPINES...
IS AN INCREDIBLE STORY.

The water of life shall
cleanse your soul,
When your soul is
cleansed - you'll hear
the call.
The call of the
Philippines - an island
of love,
Blessed as sacred -
by the good lord,
above.

The call of the lord
we hear time to time,
That's when I write
my rhyming rhyme.
To think of the islands
of love in my dreams;
'I'll always be in love -
with the beautiful
Philippines.'

Blessed are their
lives, their love, and
their sadness -
They are all so loving -
they love forgiveness.
They share their lives
which is blessed by
the lord,
The love of the
Philippines - we
welcome on board.

Fear not, said he -
who drinks the water -
For thy love is now
cleansed - as you
cleanse each other.
For thine is the
kingdom - the power
and the glory,
The love of the
Philippines - is an
incredible story.

THE BEAUTIFUL PHILIPPINES

There is a paradise so far away
That one day I'll visit and I will
stay.
A land made by God – for all
the people –
Where you and your loved one
can marry in the temple.

A land so beautiful – the sky is
so blue,
Where vegetation thrives for
me and for you.
The sea is so clear – and oh so
blue,
The people of the Philippines –
will welcome you.

The temples, and the churches,
are there to be blessed,
They welcome you all – as a very
special guest.
To marry your sweetheart – or
to christen a child,
You can also pray if you feel so
beguild.

The mountains I see, and the
villages too,
Are all there to see, for me and
for you.
Climb to the top and bless the
day,
And the lord shall answer - and
show you the way.

There's a love in the air – and
you'll feel it there,
The people there – do really
care.
A joy to be loved as never before,
Their true-love from the
Philippines, means a lot more

The wildlife too, the exotic
animals,
Just to see them – you'll get
the thrills.
All different colours – and
their love always matters,
To keep the life's circle, of
the animals quarters.

Enjoy the love and the beauty
of the Philippines –
You will even see it in your
dreams.
A beautiful paradise – for all to
see,
The beautiful Philippines – are
for you and for me.

The night time sky shines so
bright,
Even the angels sing with much
delight.
This tranquil island paradise, is
loved by all –
The beautiful Philippines – they
do enthral.

I ask you, heavenly father, to bless this land –
Please show us a sign – with your almighty hand?
To keep safe the paradise which you do love,
The Philippines you made – from heaven above.

THE BEAUTIFUL ROSES OF THE PHILIPPINES

(I dedicate this poem to all the
beautiful flowers that grow -
and thrive in the Philippines.
May God Bless Them.)

The roses of the Philippines,
are so lovely, all in rows,
They love the Philippines so
much - the rose it truly
grows.

The sun makes the energy -
the rain gives it water,
The rose starts to dance,
just like it oughta!

The flowers are blooming
beautiful, as the good
people there,
The roses are all in colour -
as they all grow with loving
care.

The clouds are of purest
white, they sail across the
sky,
They sail past the blue of
day - they are really quite
shy!

So lets all love those roses,
of the Philippines, oh so cute,

They are the flowers of the
people - who play their
tuneful flute?

The flute is the music, the
roses dance to good,
As the music sounds so
adorable - it's music sent
from God.

So bless those lovely roses,
as they bloom so lovingly
high,
They stand together, as well
they should - the roses are
now dry.

The island of the roses, are
the Philippines so pure,
Those roses are now all in
love - I just know that for sure!

THE CARER AND THE PATIENT

(My very special poem for all
you Blackpool carers - who all
do a fantastic job - but are so
very poorly paid. You all do a
fabulous - and very demanding
job. In which it really should be
more recognised and rewarded.)

The care you receive at home,
is sometimes all alone,
All you want is some dignity,
not stripping down to the
bone?

But the home that you call
home - is your castle and
your throne,
So you have the right to
have dignity, and the right
to live alone.

Not to be hassled behind
closed doors, so you fret
the whole day through,
You shouldn't have to worry
about - the care you get
under one's roof?

Home caring is demanding,
and it does take some
understanding,
When you care for a loved

one - or a patient, please
show them love and caring?

You really do need to be
a saint - as the carers do
work hard,
But they are so put upon,
especially their wages, they
really are absurd?

Some respect and gratitude,
please, the carers who all
are great,
There are mistakes - we all
know that - but the majority
are a treat!

So please take care and if
you're my carer, I'll treat
you with respect,
I'll give you treats, and I'll
be your friend - that's just
what we all expect?

THE CARERS ARE BRILLIANT

(A very special poem to pay
tribute to all the carers, and
support staff, and the house
maids, all over the world.
You really are all absolutely
fantastic. I just hope someone
in 'authority' sees this poem.
Darryl Ashton, salutes you all.)

To make someone smile
is a precious gift in style,
You can make a difference,
when all you need to do
is smile!

To watch the person's
face light-up, is a reward
in itself,
You only need to chat to
them - so they don't feel
left on the shelf!

Just to make a cuppa, or
a bacon butty,
Providing you can help
them eat, their peanut
butty, nutty?

You're a diamond in your
heart, we all know that,
And when you cook and
clean - you also have a
chat!

It makes the day seem all the better,
And when you laugh - you don't bother about the weather?

Whether you are a support nurse, a carer or a maid,
If you make that person happy - you have got it made!

These helpers are essential, and they are so much like gold,
So when they come to visit you - you just do keep a hold?

A visit, and a chat, can really make the difference,
Of feeling low and depressed, and it lifts their own self confidence.

So let us all salute the carers, who are a valuable asset,
Cos come one day - you never know - you could be the target?

Around the world, too, the carers do so special,
Their loyalty, and friendship, are absolutely essential.

I have good friends on the
Facebook, from all around
the world,
And their work is just amazing -
I'd raise their pay if I could!

So let us all salute the carers,
who work so magnificent,
And in our hearts - we know
it's true - their worth 100%.

THE CLOSING SEASON OF WORLD FOOTBALL

The football season is
closing, and the teams
are doing battle – with
their own salvation,
Some are fighting
relegation – some are
hoping for promotion.
All over Europe – be it
France, Spain or
Germany,
Even in Italy – they
start their football
journey.

The highs and lows
of the football clubs,
Some are celebrating
in the pubs.
But some are in tears
as they face their
greatest fears,
Being relegated – it all
ends up in tears.

In Europe and beyond –
football is the game,
In America they also
play it – soccer is the
name.
For every boy wants

to be a brilliant football
star,
And if they do keep
on winning – they know
they've WON the war!

And let's not forget
the managers – who
really are stressed out.
Constantly making
their decisions – even
if in doubt.
The fans too play a big
part – they cheer their
team to win.
And then they go to
the bar – for a swift'
large tasty GIN!

I have NO doubt that
in my mind the game
is all about money.
And the English Premier
League – is the league
of milk and honey.
It is were the money
really is – and every
team wants to be there.
But you really have to
be brilliant – the money
is the lure!

There is great wealth
in the football game –

this is oh so true,
There's a lot of
entertainment – for me
and for you.
The season is a long
one – and players do
get injured.
But they always do
recover – and play on
so unhindered!

So, who will be promoted?
and who will be relegated?
The moment of truth is
closing in – it soon will be
decided.
Good luck to all the teams
who are fighting for their
lives,
Always have faith – and
say a prayer – and you
may get a nice surprise!

Good luck to everyone of
you – I mean that all so
true.
There are quite a few clubs
struggling – but soon you'll
feel brand new!
The end of the season is
fast approaching – let the
battle now commence.
The joys of 'WORLD FOOTBALL'
– is full of excitement and
suspense.

HAPPY 25th BIRTHDAY TO SKY SPORTS

Happy Birthday to Sky
Sports,
You show all sports and
of all sorts.
The football world is shown
to us,
Through a box – and cutting
the fuss.
Happy Birthday to Sky
Sports.
But I will never wear my
shorts!
The English Premier
League does shine.
On Sky Sports as some
do whine.

There are pundits galore,
getting well paid.
But why aren't they all
managing – are they
afraid?
Sky do dominate that's
for sure.
Paying huge money they
know it's a cure.
But beware dear people –
you'll pay for sure!
The bosses are cheering
their birthday today.
Happy 25th birthday – to
you today.

But what surprises have
Sky Sports got planned?
What I really should doing
is watching; Grandstand!!!!!
Here's a surprise for all
our subscribers,
We want more money –
and lots of new TENERS!
Yes, the monthly fee is
now going up.
Maybe we should sign a
football prenup!
A birthday party for the
bosses,
But sometimes they do –
count their losses!

Happy Birthday to Sky
Sports.
Another 25 years – in
cavorts.
But the fee just keeps
rising – and some folk
have left.
Feeling 'ripped off' – and
so bereft.
It's all about money –
and power and greed.
Happy Birthday to Sky
Sports – I mean that
indeed!

LEICESTER CITY: THE CHAMPIONS OF THE ENGLISH PREMIER LEAGUE

There is a football team
in the English Premier League,
They are defying all the odds – causing so much intrigue.
They've hardly lost all season long,
They're at the top –
where they do belong.

Defying all the odds,
and playing at their best,
Every game they play –
they rise up to the test.
They play just like a dream – and play with skill and more,
And all the fans applaud them – especially when they score!

They really are the envy,
of the other football clubs,
They are second to none, they even have super subs!!!!
They play to a packed

house – and their football
is a delight,
Everyone does their bit –
with winning in their
sight.

The manager has done
a remarkable job, what
a team they are.
They've won most of
their games – and now
they will go far.
A dream of dreams is
all too clear, and the
trophy they do chase.
Sitting firmly on the
top – their position
they do embrace.

A remarkable season
they have had – as
they enter the final run.
And moving ever closer –
to being the Number
ONE!
Sitting there as proud
as punch, they show us
all intrigue,
May I present Leicester
City – the champions of
the English Premier
League

THE BRILLIANCE OF ACCRINGTON STANLEY

Well done to Accrington
Stanley, you really are playing well,
And sooner or later – in
Division One you will
surely dwell

Your rise up Division
Two is absolutely
remarkable,
Now winning deserved
promotion – is now
very possible.

The manager has
done wonders – and
so has the owner,
All the players are
fabulous – always
shoulder to shoulder.

Out on that football
pitch – and playing
super footy,
Then come half time –
they enjoy a 'BIG' mug
of tea!

But what is their
secret, of their players
playing like silk?
'That's right. You've
guessed it – they're
still drinking all that
milk!!!!

It is obviously working,
the players are all
transformed.
They're playing better
than ever – a super
team, they've formed.

Accrington is a small
town – but it has a
fabulous football team.
Climbing up the Division
Two – it really is a
dream!

Let's all applaud them.
as they march on to
win promotion;
'The brilliant Accrington
Stanley – they play with
such devotion.'

I wonder what food they
eat – or, is that a BIG
surprise?
'I bet they go to the
market – and buy some
Oddies pies!'

Oddies pies and milk,
blimey, no wonder
they're playing well.
Just keep this up you
lads, you hear, the
pies and milk does
gel!

The fans are all behind
you – as so is the
whole of Lancashire.
And when you win
promotion – this moment
you all will treasure.

I know I speak for the
whole of Accrington –
as it is the truth, you
see;
'Let's tell the world of
a super team – the
brilliance of Accrington
Stanley.'

THE LOWER ECHELONS OF ENGLISH FOOTBALL

Blackpool football club
are trying their best,
To play good football –
and pass the test.
They slowly climb up
the very high table,
Winning some games –
and now they are
stable.

The Oyston's won't
buy and spend any
cash,
This causes friction –
even a rash!
The fans aren't happy –
that is true,
They voice their anger
at the privileged few!

Little Fleetwood Town,
they've slipped up.
They've lost their form
and won't win the cup.
They did play well – and
won each game,
But now they're struggling –
who is to blame?

They are close to the
bottom – and they do
fear,
But they'll start winning –
and then we'll all cheer!
They started so well –
but now they do struggle,
But, they'll get better –
they're just in a muddle!

But the team doing well,
is Accrington Stanley,
In Division Two – they
sit there patiently.
They are playing well –
and that is so true,
Fans turn up – and there's
always a queue!

Two players sent off – but
the team rallied round.
They played their hearts
out – holding their ground.
Drinking their milk – it
does them all good.
They are winning more
games – as they know
they should.

The lower league's are
doing good – and deserve
a mention.
They play good football –
it is a suggestion.

Their aim is to win – and
hopefully win promotion.
Then all the fans can sing
the tuneful; 'locomotion!'

So hail the lower teams
who are paid so much
less.
Some have other jobs –
and part time, I do guess.
They are entertaining –
that is for sure.
They all want to win –
run around, and score!

THE PROBLEMS AT MANCHESTER UNITED

The reign of Louis Van
Gaal, is now almost over,
Does this mean Jose
Mourinho – will almost
certainly be in clover?

The fans have all had
enough – and Louis
Van Gaal fears his reign
is now all over.
So will Van Gaal be on
the ferry – departing now
from Dover!

The Manchester United
board have now made
their BIG decision,
Will Van Gaail now be
ousted – by the Man
United inquisition!
He tried his best but
it wasn't enough,
Time will now surely
tell – if Van Gaal has
lost the stuff!!!!

The ending is now nigh,
as a new messiah, they
now hunt.

56

Who could that person
be? Is a "SPECIAL" one
in front?
I know they still miss
Ferguson – and they'd
love to have him back;
'But a very "SPECIAL"
personality – is about to
have a crack!'

Enter Jose Mourinho –
who used to be boss
at Chelsea,
Maybe he will relish
the challenge – we'll
all have to wait and
see!

He brought success to
Stamford Bridge, that
we all know well.
So will he take over
at Man U – and success,
they may all dwell.

The football world is
a rocky one – and always
full of surprises.
Sackings and signings –
all come in all sorts of
disguises.
But there's always the
mega money – that goes
with all the winning;
'And even in the news

media – the gossip they
are all spinning!'

Manchester United have
struggled – they've really
found it hard,
I bet all those players
have trained well – even
in their own back yard!
Their glory years have
halted – but this they all
do know;
'Can the "SPECIAL" one
save Man U – in the form
of Jose Mourinho?

WHAT IS HAPPENING AT LIVERPOOL FOOTBALL CLUB?

Liverpool football club, have
now got so very greedy,
They should be reducing
their tickets – for the poor
and the needy.
To make a quick buck or
two – which is what they
all do think,
But hiking up the costs
again – can cause a great
"BIG" stink!

The fans walked out on
Liverpool – showing their
disgust.
Walking home in anger –
their bad tempers they
did thrust.
The ticket prices now have
rocketed – not only at
Liverpool –
Why are they doing this –
do they think it's cool?

Yes, they pay high wages,
and the price of tickets
cover this;
'But some of us live in
poverty, not a life of bliss!'
I bet there are other clubs –
who are doing the same.

They really should reduce
their tickets – and stop
causing such a shame.'

Football is a business, but
greed has grasped a hold,
Hiking up the price of
tickets – they do need to
be told.
Is it too late? Will Liverpool
fans forgive?
The cynical move by the
Liverpool club – the fans are
not to give!

But, why is there all this
greed, in the name of football?
Greedy directors – and even
agents – they all hear the
money call!
A good day out for the family –
what no one can afford.
The inflated prices to see a
match – and they want us all
on board!

'So, please, you greedy football
clubs – think about your fans,
Not everyone earns mega-money –
and can sit in luxury, in the stands.'
'Please, reduce your ticket prices –
and don't act like greedy MPs;
'Or sometime in the future – you'll
be 'capped' to a "ticket-price"
"FREEZE!"'

THE JOYS AND PLEASURES OF PREMIER LEAGUE FOOTBALL

The English Premier League
is full of woes and more,
 All the classy footballers –
 want to really score.
On the pitch they flash their skill –
and also their anger,
 Especially those strikers –
In my day it was called:
 'goal-hanger!'

Even on a crisp cold day
they always wear their
gloves,
And all the fans upon the
stands – they're chanting
in their droves.
The manager's are in their
dugout – looking so bemused,
Glancing at their substitutes –
will any of them be used?

There is also BIG MONEY in
the beautiful game of ours –
As all the Premier footballers
all drive their flashy cars.
They all work hard and play
hard – and they enjoy a beer
in the pub.
They also enjoy their dancing –
in a London' West End
"erotic-style" night club!!!!

Their career is a short one –
so they have to earn their
money,
and if they are all married –
they give money to their
honey.
Some do go off the rails –
that is a fact.
but most of the footballers
always play with tact.

Sometimes there is trouble,
and bad language is a
concern.
So if you want to "EFFING"
swear a lot – please do wait
your turn!!!!
There is also discipline – and
the punishment is tough.
Then the manager's ask their
players; 'have you had enough?'

Yes, they also spit a lot – and
it doesn't look so nice.
But that's because of the bad
taste – of their smelly' Old Spice!
They run around like cattle –
as they chase the ball;
'Scattering here – and over
there – as they hear the call.'

On occasions they do dive a
lot – to try and "CON" the ref.
Just to get a free kick – or a
penalty; 'they hold their breath!'

They run up and down the pitch –
fighting for the ball.
And when they lose their temper –
they feel a angry call!

Other countries too – they do have
super players.
I wonder before every game;
'do they all say prayers?'
"Help us lord to grasp this game –
and no kicking on the shin.
All we want to do today – is
hopefully always WIN!"

Then they are ready – and able
to play first class;
'But due to the slippery grass –
some fall on their AS*!!!!'
They've heard the call from
the lord – who shouts his
orders true;
'Go and tackle them – you swabs –
as he badly needs the loo!'

The teams are on the pitch –
as the ref does introduce.
'They cannot wait for halftime,
to drink their orange juice.'
The game of footy is a good
one – full of wacky surprises.
But why do they still kiss each
other – to express their own
vices?

No matter where in the world,
you play your football match,
The game is always better –
when you start from scratch.
Enjoy the English Premier
League – on a cold and wet
Saturday,
And when your team score a
goal – you can all shout…
HOORAY!!!!

JOHN TERRY: SHOULD I LEAVE – OR SHOULD I CALL THEIR BLUFF?

My name is John Terry,
and I really have had
enough,
I want to leave Chelsea
football club – 'or do I
call their bluff?'
I came here when I was
fourteen – or, somewhere
in between,
I want to see the world –
if you know what I mean!

Stamford Bridge has been
my home for such a very
long time,
I've played a lot of games
here – I've seen changes
so sublime!
I want to go to pastures
new – and enhance my
skills even more;
'I'd like play till I'm fifty,
blimey, now that I will
adore!'

I have played alongside the
best – and seen some new
faces,
We always get together –
and have a bet on the races!
We all train very hard – we
do have such high standards.

If we win our game – we
have a drink afterwards!

We have a new owner – he
spends a lot of money.
He buys all the best talent –
never no one phony!
Sadly, we lost Jose Mourinho –
he left the club he loved.
But the players rebelled
against him – so out the
door he was shoved!

I am leaving after this season,
but I have to now move on.
To proudly march forward –
Maybe play football in the
sun!
I don't want an English club –
a change is what I need.
I want to broaden my
horizons, a change from the
English Premier League!

Maybe I can join my mate,
my good friend Frank Lampard.
He plays in America – and
he also plays so hard.
Maybe that's my destiny –
to America, I may go?
Playing along side Frank
Lampard – we could put on a
show!

My time at Chelsea is now
all over – time for pastures
new.
I'm not getting any younger –
but this I always knew!
I have also played for England,
and scored a good few
goals.
I also did captain Chelsea –
I was proud – and it always
shows!

I leave Chelsea football club,
with my head held high;
'Another chapter in my life,
this I can't deny.'
Will I go to America? Or,
will I stay in the UK?
Maybe I'll go to Spain – or
somewhere far, far away!

I fancy getting some sun –
Dubai would be nice.
But they aren't BIG on
football – so maybe I'll
think twice!
No matter were I go – it
will be a brand new start
for me;
'I'm leave Chelsea football
club – my name is; 'John
Terry".

JOHN TERRY: THE DILEMMA OF A CHELSEA FOOTBALL

My name is John Terry,
and I can't make my
mind up –
I want to play for
Chelsea – and win the
Premier League Cup.
There has been some
speculation – if I'm
leaving London town,
But I really don't know
what to do – and I wear
a frown!

I played alongside
Drogba – and my good
friend, Frank Lampard;
'When we had baths
together – we'd wear
a leotard!'
I really don't know
what to do – my career
is almost over!
I want to stay at Chelsea –
and feel all in clover.

My wages are NOT an
issue – but a pay rise
would be nice.
And playing on the footy
pitch – smelling of Old

Spice!!!!
I wouldn't mind a pay
rise – maybe £300.000
per week.
But if I asked for that
amount – it would be a
bloody cheek!

I have to consider my
future – and my family;
'Maybe I can go to division
two – and play for
Accrington Stanley!'
No, they don't need me –
they are dong well,
Maybe I can go to
Fleetwood Town – I'm
sure I would gel.

Or maybe even Blackpool –
and help them to climb
the league,
it really would be a
challenge, and create lots
of intrigue!
But, there is just one big
problem – they can't afford
my wages.
I could play for free – but
I've not done that in ages.

I want to go to the sun,
somewhere were it's warm,
Play my footy in the sun,

and use my cockney charm!
I could play for Dubai – for
the Arabian knights,
And meet old Alibaba – and
hail their footy rights!!!!

I have loved my time at
Chelsea – but my future is
now in doubt.
I will consult my agent – he
is a talent scout!
Whether or not I do leave,
my beloved Chelsea FC,
And move to pastures new –
all will be revealed on the
news – especially on TV!

I have to make a decision,
as I am now getting old.
But, like a lot of other
players; 'I hate doing what
I'm told!'
'Will I say goodbye?' 'Or,
will I stay at Chelsea?'
'It all depends what's on the
table – "mega wages", all
for me!!!!'

WHAT HAS HAPPENED TO MANCHESTER UNITED?

What has happened to
Manchester United?
Their once brilliant play
has since departed!
From the days when
they were so brilliant,
Now they are struggling –
and it shows, so evident.

Louis Van Gaal is now
under pressure,
To start winning games,
and to reassure.
The stars of today are
all well paid,
But their skills on the
pitch – sometimes does
fade.

Wayne Rooney, is
suffering to,
He has to improve – or
retire with the crew.
Other players too – must
come together,
Support their manager –
who's at the end of his
tether!

Old Trafford should be buzzing with trophies to show,
But at this moment – they all do feel low.
What can they do? What is the answer?
How can they win – their sparkle – to recapture?

The media are watching – that is for sure,
Winning their games – is the right cure.
To come together – and play like they can,
Play for their manager – Van Gaal, is their man.

They are suffering now – and time is the boss,
All their talent – is it a loss?
They must improve – and start to win;
'Or their manager is out – that is a sin.'

Other teams too – they also do suffer,
The winter is harsh – they must back each other.
To reproduce their glory days –

But at the moment – they're
all in a daze.

The Busby babes – now
they were good,
And, even Ron Atkinson –
tall, he stood!
But Alex Ferguson, he
was the master,
Winning trophies galore,
avoiding disaster!

Several owners have
cause for concern,
American's now – money,
they burn.
The Glazers are sweating –
as the pay role is gigantic,
Watching their future – the
buck is erratic!

Louis Van Gaal, he sure
is sweating,
Maybe Old Trafford is now
all fretting.
Just have more faith – and
believe in your team;
'And victory will come – you
know what I mean?'

We wish you luck and you'll
all come through,
Old Trafford will buzz – I
mean that so true.

Good luck to Man United,
I say that with a smile;
'Let's all back their manager,
Louis Van Gaal.'

BLACKPOOL vs WEST HAM -
A RE-CREATION

Come on you players' you can do it,
Said manager Ian Holloway.
Go out there and do your stuff,
Run around and act real tough!

As the ref did blow his whistle loud,
All the singing came from the crowd.
This really was a joy to hear,
Come on you Blackpool get in gear.

Crainey and Evatt passed the ball,
Then slipped it to Ince, who heard the call
Then passed the ball to Taylor-Fletcher,
Who slot it home right past the keeper!

Then off again they did go,
Looking again to score more goals.
Stephen Dobbie controlled the ball,
And 'hammered' it in – to the open goal.

Then Philips ran with the ball,
He heard a shout: 'Hey, pass the ball?'
Philips looked up and saw Ormerod close,
Passed it to him – and Ormerod scores!

Blackpool are now 'two-nil' up,
And they are playing like a Premier Club.
The hammers themselves have been out played,
Now Blackpool can venture on their victory parade!

What a team, and what a game,
But credit to the players – what a dream.
But the man in charge and who changed the club,
Is Ian Holloway – who's down the pub!

A TICKET FOR THE MATCH

My boss sent me an E-mail
I haven't answered yet.
I'm sure it was important,
As important as they get.

My boss will not be happy,
He'll foam, he'll fume and glower,
But I've a ticket for the match
That kicks off in an hour.

"You ought to do some shopping,"
Calls out my irate wife,
"There's nothing left for us to eat,
No bread, no cheese, no rice.

We need some fruit, we need some veg,
Some eggs, some milk, some flour,
But I've a ticket for the match
That kicks off in an hour.

I glance at the newspaper,
It's full of tales of woe:
War in Iraq, knife-attacks,
Share prices sinking low.

I know we should protest
and do
Whatever's in my power,
But I've a ticket for the
match
That kicks off in an hour.

I'm out the house and in
the street,
I'm rushing to the ground,
My pulse-rate's shifted up
a gear,
My heart's begun to pound.

Looks like a storm's about
to break,
Overhead thick, dark clouds
lower,
Still, I've a ticket for the
match
That kicks off in an hour.

A streetwalker waylays me
And gives me the glad eye.
Says: "Come up to my
boudoir, pal,
I'll show you a real good
time."

Now, the prospect's quite
inviting,
She's pretty as a flower,
But I'd much rather see the
match
That kicks off in an hour.

At last I'm at the stadium,
I'm all set to go in,
Then, the steward checks my ticket,
Then informs me with a grin…

"I'm sorry, mate, you're somewhat late,
Perhaps your watch is slow,
This match you bought a ticket for
Kicked off an hour ago!"

ALEKSANDR ORLOV AND SERGEI PLAY MEERKAT FOOTBALL

My name is Aleksandr
Orlov, and I am now
a meerkat footballer,
I cannot play in the
goal – because I need
to be taller!
I will be the referee,
and Sergei will be in
goal –
Oleg will be meerkat
striker – but he cannot
get the ball?

We are playing in the
England – in the English
Premier League –
Where all the footballers
are very rich – I have
to join indeed.
Playing also in the USA –
and scoring lots of goals,
Sergei is no good – he
always has to crawls!!!!

But, we are the meerkat
professionals – and we
have to play the same,
But if I do not score any
goal – Sergei I will blame.
Off we run onto the pitch –
it is so real grass,

But Sergei looks so daft
in shorts – he's such a
silly ass!!!!

We like the O-Posts –
super blog – they like our
writing friend,
Hello to Sir Darryl Ashton –
he writes a brand new
trend.
We love to play in America –
we feel like movie stars,
But Sergei tries to kiss me –
when I'm watching the
Star Wars!!!!

We also play the soccer – in
sunny Africa –
I run all over the hot land –
we need to drink more
water.
The Meerkat's will play
England – for a silver solid
cup,
But Oleg cannot play today –
he is just a pup!!
Sergei thinks he's the best –
I let him down gently –
He's too old, and far too
slow – he used to run so
speedy!

We have to get real – and
we cannot play the soccer –

We leave that to the humans –
then I give them all a lecture.
Sergei likes the football – and
he plays with his furry pimple –
Now he watches on meerkat
TV – it's all incredibly SIMPLE!!!!

We have to be professional –
and not act like we're smoothies,
Being in the English Football
Premier League – is better
than Hollywood Movies.

We do not like to kiss each
other – we shake our claws
to celebrate –
It just doesn't look right –
Sergei knows his fate!!!!

We will always be the better
team – but Sergei is now a
slob;
'Being in charge of IT – and
playing his computermabob!!!!'
So, now we watch the football,
on large screen television –
Welcome to meerkat football –
now it's intermission!!!!!!

MANCHESTER UNITED IN CRISIS

Manchester United aren't
doing too well,
This is evident – as one
can tell.
Louis Van Gaal is now
under pressure,
Will the players respond –
for good measure?

They are now struggling,
to win their matches –
This has prompted an
Old Trafford crisis.
The players are not as
good as they were,
They all get well paid –
so, do they care?

It is the season to be

festive,
But the players do note;
'will they forgive?'
Will Louis Van Gaal be
sacked by the owners?
Then Manchester United
will seek Mourinho's
favours!

The gossip is rife – as

the blues march on –
Will Manchester United
recruit the 'special one?'
It's a funny old world at
the moment in football,
Will Jose Mourinho get
the call?

The Premier League is
so full of footballing
woes,
Football managers' are
sacked – anything goes!
'Why do the players rebel
like they don't give a hoot?
They should all be told;
'or they'll all get the boot!'

There seems to be friction
between some players,
Is this when the player's
all discuss their careers?
It seems no one is exempt
from getting the boot,
But, they don't seem to
care – with all that loot!

One manager will go –
another will arrive,
I think that football will
no doubt survive.
Fear not says the ref –

for he's in sole charge;
'That is a 'foul' – not a
'shoulder-like' barge!'

Welcome to the world of
football my friends,
It is here were you'll see
whole new trends.
My players aren't playing,
what shall I do?
Just wait for your fate;
'by the boardroom crew!!!!'

JOSE MOURINHO – SACKED A WEEK BEFORE CHRISTMAS

'Twas the week before Christmas,
and Chelsea are doomed,
Sacking their manager – Mourinho,
they fumed!

The boardroom were ruthless,
he has to go,
And off he went – the prodigal
Mourinho!'

The 'special one' just gazed
as he was read the last rites,
But he didn't care – it wasn't
a surprise!

A lady physio – was jumping
for joy,
She'd won her battle – Jose,
to destroy!

The players all wept as they
lost their hero,
Jose Mourinho – they called;
'Captain Nemo!'

'The Chelsea club was now
in trouble,
Who would help them? They're
trapped in a bubble!

The blues are definitely all
singing the blues,
But why are they all dancing –
on hearing this news?'

The boardroom will pay him
a massive big fee,
But Mourinho shrugs it all off –
and heads home for his tea.

'Chelsea are chasing a guy
called; Van Gaal,
From Manchester United –
will he hear their call?'

The game of football is so
full of woes,
Anything is possible – anything
goes!

The special one is no more –
as he heads out the door,
His mega fat wages – Mourinho,
does adore.

The owners have seen the
last of him now;
But Mourinho will be chuckling;
'he's the special one', somehow!'

The players are gathering to
meet their new gaffer,
But who should come in – with
a clank and a clatter!

Yes, Mourinho is Santa – he
shouts: 'Ho! Ho! Ho!
He's now gone to Lapland
with his elves, well in tow!

He turns to Chelsea and grins
like a king,
With ten million quid – oh, I will
wear some bling!

So now it's all over – It's
goodbye to Chelsea;
'Will they play better – we'll
just wait and see!'

'Merry Christmas I say – as I
feel no dismay;
'I've got "ten million pounds"
– "hip-pip"…hooray!!!!'

ENGLAND – THE UNDERDOGS OF EURO 2016

England are the underdogs,
that is plain to see,
They're in the Euro 2016 –
and Rooney's hurt his knee!
We never seem to do well –
and we never win a trophy,
Will we win this competition –
and revel in the glory?

We all stick together, and
play our very best,
But, sadly, as we all do know –
we always fail the test.
We are manged by Roy
Hodgson – who is always
in command,
But on occasions we do
play naff – and he grabs
us by the hand.

We only just qualified –
that is the shocking
truth,
So, if we do ever win a
game, we may feel so
uncouth!
We are to play Wales,
the country of song and

voice,
But if England do beat
them – the world will
all rejoice!

We must be all positive –
and hail the England
football team,
But, sadly, at the moment –
winning is just a dream.
Maybe we can enlist some
help – especially for free;
'How about little Fleetwood
Town – or even Accrington
Stanley!!!!'

England need to concentrate
and be more positive,
Our cynicism they will
forgive.
Take each game as it
comes – like the side of
1966,
They should look to the
future – there is no quick
fix!!

We must play like we are
"world class" – and hold
our heads up high,
Because if we fail again –
we'll all be hung out to
dry!!!!
Our manager's, too, they

need to pick all the very best players,
Or, we'll end up like Paul Gascoigne – it'll all end in a flood of tears!

So, come on you England – do your duty, do it for the Queen,
Go to Euro 2016 – show everyone you're mean!!!!
With your heads held high, you all stand proud, and you want to "kiss your teammate"!
Show the world we are "superstars" – or we'll quickly know our fate!

But let us look to the future – as we all have had enough.
What the England football team really needs is; ' a manager like Sir Brian Clough.'
So, hail, hail, and hail again, will England win the day?
Only if they are managed by; 'the ghost of Sir Alf Ramsay.

THE WORLD CUP COULD BE AN ALIEN NATION

The World Cup is a trophy
that every player wants to
win,
Even if it means kicking a
player – right on his already
bruised shin!
It is a trophy of solid Gold –
and is loved by every player,
Every four years it arrives –
the football world's in top
gear!

Many nations do compete –
the prize awaits the best.
Playing in the groups they
do – the ultimate playing
test.
From all around the globe –
country's do compete,
All the world class players –
running on their feet.

From South America – to
Europe too – and even in
another galaxy,
The world cup finals are
watched in space – by an
alien large society!
Yes, my friends, Star Trek
is out there – they love the

U.S. soccer –
Together they watch in outer
space – it couldn't get any better!

The world cup is a dream –
as the martians do enjoy;
'They play the game of
football – like it is a toy!'
Even the Champions League –
is known in outer space,
The martians are so very
skillful – they admire the
human race.

The space is in total darkness,
but there's a match being
played tonight,
Is it the martian' World Cup –
or a "Trick or Treat" delight?
Our game of football is now
known – even in deepest
space;
'The martians enjoy our world
cup – as we play with so much grace.'

So, as the world teams do
battle – for a prize of glory,
Is the space game so surreal –
or just another story?
The World Cup and the
Champions League – are all
prestige' sporting competitions,
Even if we're being watched –
by martian's from an alien-
being' space galaxy nations!!!!

THE GOLDEN BOOT OF FOOTBALL AWARD

The golden boot of football,
is given only to a select few,
So if you surely want one –
you must now join a queue.
This award is an honour –
and it salutes the player's
ability,
The golden football boot
award – is also internationally.

The golden football boot
ward – is a prize to hold
and cherish,
The only thing you cannot
do is smother the boot in polish!
Every player drools, and
would love to own this boot –
But you really have to be
exceptional – and wear a
very smart suit.

It really is a privilege to
hold up high this award,
Everyone does want it – but
you have to be a soccer
lord.
The golden football boot,
is a special prize for sure,
Only the cream of the crop,
can feel the boot's amour.

So let us see the players –
who tend to win this as a
big surprise.
When they lift the golden
boot – tears do fill their eyes.
From England through to
the Europe greats – and also
far and wide,
Every football player in the
world today – this football
boot we abide.

So, who will seek this golden
boot out – and cherish it
for ever?
Whoever is awarded it – it
will be their true endeavour.
From world cup greats – the
list is there – all the players'
now on board:
'Ladies and gentleman I ask
you now – who'll win the
golden football boot award?'

THE MAGIC OF A TIMELESS
ENGLISH LANDMARK

The football players I see at the Wembley Stadium,
looking so splendour,
It invites me to look closer –
the magic I will capture?
The stadium is so awesome,
it feels fit for a king,
And when I move even
closer – I even start to sing!

I see the Wembley Stadium,
it really does look grand,
I have to get even closer –
and listen to the band.
It is a fabulous stadium, as
legend already knows,
The home of internationals –
and where the fans all roars.

The magic Wembley Stadium,
is a sight to behold,
Many teams have been
privileged – a story to be told?
England have played there –
and also Scotland, too,
Even Wales and Ireland – all
are in the queue!

All the world class teams have

graced this awesome stadium,
Brazil and also Germany –
and Holland is the spectrum.
South America are also there –
with Argentina and Chile,
All have played at Wembley –
a privilege of duty.

So the magic that is Wembley,
the stadium of football,
You may get the chance to
play there – but you have to
score a goal!
From Wembley Stadium, we
welcome you – to watch these
world class teams,
Where you can see the stars
in action – and not only in your
dreams.

knew – were the cream of
the crop.
And when they went on the
pitch – we'd see who came
out on top?
I remember Francis Lee,
and Mike Summerbee,
Then came Colin Bell,
who all played for
Manchester City.

Even the Arsenal – now
they also were the stunners.
From Charlie George – to

Pat Jennings – they were
the brilliant' Gunners!
At Highbury they played –
every match an epic,
Even their manager –
George Graham was a
tonic!

Leeds United were also
there, all dressed in
virginal white.
All their brilliant players –
a magical delight.
From Billy Bremner, to
Peter Lorimar – and Allan
Clarke, too,
They really were a dynamic
team – one heck of a crew!

All the teams of the golden
years – so many I could
name,
They all played so brilliant –
at their chosen game.
Kevin Keegan and John
Toshack – and also Jimmy
Greaves,
They all were simply
superb – they had magic
up their sleeves!!!!

And even when it was
snowing – the lads would
all stall play,

They ran about all over the
place – they simply enjoyed
their day.
The fans all cheered – and
some really swore,
But everyone enjoyed
themselves – then a player
would often score!!!!

The magic days out at the
football match, really was a
treat,
The players all entertaining
us – the ball was at their
feet.
The final whistle was then
blown, and everyone just
cheered,
Then before the arrival of
health and safety – the
grounds were carefully
cleared.

The golden years of the
football teams – and the
football players,
We idolised all the greats –
and we even shed some
tears!
Now we move forward to
a whole new generation –
and start a new found
nation;
'What a fabulous sport we
do have – our football team's creation?'

THE FOOTBALL PLAYERS
THAT I ONCE KNEW

The football players I once
knew – were the cream of
the crop.
And when they went on the
pitch – we'd see who came
out on top?
I remember Francis Lee,
and Mike Summerbee,
Then came Colin Bell,
who all played for
Manchester City.

Even the Arsenal – now
they also were the stunners.
From Charlie George – to
Pat Jennings – they were
the brilliant' Gunners!
At Highbury they played –
every match an epic,
Even their manager –
George Graham was a
tonic!

Leeds United were also
there, all dressed in
virginal white.
All their brilliant players –
a magical delight.
From Billy Bremner, to
Peter Lorimar – and Allan

Clarke, too,
They really were a dynamic
team – one heck of a crew!

All the teams of the golden
years – so many I could
name,
They all played so brilliant –
at their chosen game.
Kevin Keegan and John
Toshack – and also Jimmy
Greaves,
They all were simply
superb – they had magic
up their sleeves!!!!

And even when it was
snowing – the lads would
all stall play,
They ran about all over the
place – they simply enjoyed
their day.
The fans all cheered – and
some really swore,
But everyone enjoyed
themselves – then a player
would often score!!!!

The magic days out at the
football match, really was a
treat,
The players all entertaining
us – the ball was at their
feet.

The final whistle was then blown, and everyone just cheered,
Then before the arrival of health and safety – the grounds were carefully cleared.

The golden years of the football teams – and the football players,
We idolised all the greats – and we even shed some tears!
Now we move forward to a whole new generation – and start a new found nation;
'What a fabulous sport we do have – our football team's creation?'

BECKS TO THE FUTURE

'Father dear,' said Romeo in 2022,
'What team shall I play for,
Now I'm grown like you?
Should I play for Real Madrid
Or should it be Manyou?'

'Why not play for Crewe?'
Mrs Becks walked in and said:
'Why not play for who?'

'Oh my gosh,' said Becks to Posh,
'I thought you were in Venice.'
'I was, but now I'm back in Britain
For a game of tennis.'

'Mother dear,' said Romeo,
'Sit down with us here.
The three of us can now discuss
My footballing career.

'Now tell me, my dear parents,
If I play in attack
'What number should be printed
On the Beckham back?'

'Well my little angel,
If you want to play in Heaven
'Where your father's dreams were made,

Why not number seven?'

'But mother dear,' said Romeo,
'When father off to Spain did flee
'In Madrid, what Daddy did
was wear a twenty – three.'

Mrs Becks and Romeo
both looked round at Daddy.
It was Mrs B who spoke
and uttered to her hubby:

'David let us know, the number,
that you recommend for our dear
Romeo.'
David Beckham cleared his throat
and croaked those words we've
grown to know:

'Wear Four out there, Romeo.'

SUCKING ON MY THUMB
SCORING FOR THE HAMMERS

I am a Premier League footballer –
and sometime's I feel numb,
And every time I score a goal –
I tend to suck my thumb!
I play for West Ham United, also
known as 'the Hammers',
But when I start to suck my
thumb – my team mates get
the jitters!!

I must admit it makes a change
from all the constant snogging;
'So as I now suck my thumb –
I've also started jogging!'
It takes me back to nursery
school – when I was just a
child,
Every time I sucked my thumb –
it drove the nurses wild!!

Even on the playing pitch – and
the weather is oh so shocking,
I'd tend to run about too much –
showing off my skin-tight
stocking!
We would also carry our mobile
phones – and send a text to our
girlfriends,
But when I'm sucking on my
thumb – I'm starting brand new

trends!

I play my football skillfully – and
we have a lot of fun,
And then in the winter – I jet
off to get some sun.
I fly to warmer climates – as the
UK's cold numbs my bum,
But I always will feel much
better – when I'm sucking on
my thumb!!!!

My name is Dimitri Payet, and
I play for West Ham United,
I scored two great wonder
goals – and got so very excited.
I started celebrating – and my
team mates grabbed my bum,
And all that excitement – it made
me suck my thumb!!!!

THE FOOTBALL WORLD HELPS THE REFUGEES

We are the refugees, we
really need your assistance,
We are fleeing persecution –
as we sail to a new existence.
We are leaving our danger
land – it is known as
Syria –
Our lives have all been torn
apart – causing mass hysteria.

But, wait, there's breaking
news; 'a land of football
stars',
They are playing football
and some do play guitars!
The Europe teams have
united – and their aim is
charity –
To help all the poor people –
known as a refugee.

Even the English Premier
League – they too are raising
money,
To help us to our new life –
on our perilous journey.
From Liverpool to Everton,
from Bournemouth and also
Chelsea,
We also love Manchester

United – and their rivals –
Manchester City!

They along with Barcelona –
and Real Madrid together,
Inter Milan and A.C. Milan –
they always get good
weather!
The fantastic teams we
all do see – is a treat for us
all, so please;
'Thank you from our hearts
and souls – as we are the
football refugees.'

A TRIBUTE TO BOTH SIR BOBBY CHARLTON AND WAYNE ROONEY

Wayne Rooney has equalled
a record, and made football
history,
He equalled his England goal
scoring – to add to his own
tally.
This record was previously
held by Sir Bobby Charlton,
And what did seem to Rooney,
it must have been a marathon!

Both of these players have
links to Manchester United,
And both of these super
players – their goals were so
invited.
The brilliant Sir Bobby Charlton,
he played for a super team,
The players of years gone by –
they really were a dream.

But Manchester United have
struggled so of late,
Was the goal by Wayne Rooney –
seen as football fate?
Rooney is a different player –
that is evident –
Bobby Charlton was world class –
he really was a gent!

The players of today – no matter
what their team,
Playing in the England football
team – is their biggest dream.
Back in the 1970s – and the 1980s,
footballers never wore gloves,
Except for the goalkeeper – they
really took the shoves!

Wayne Rooney is the highest
goal scorer – that is now the
case,
But being the all time England's
best player – Sir Bobby Charlton
was real ace!
Sir Bobby has one achievement –
which Wayne Rooney will never
better,
Sir Bobby Charlton won the world
cup – and he has this title forever.

But, well done anyway – to the
footballer Wayne Rooney,
He hangs on in there – and collects
his loadsa money!!!!
I think the world cup will always
evade the England team,
But, congratulations to Wayne
Rooney; 'you've achieved your
perfect dream.'

MANCHESTER UNITED: THE RED DEVILS OF YESTERYEAR

We really love our football
and we watch it on TV,
We like to watch the English
Premier League – but sadly
it isn't free!
The top teams are in action –
and they show a lot of skill,
But they don't like playing
in Winter time in case they
catch a chill!

Let's go back some decades
and marvel at some players,
Bobby Charlton played midfield –
and he could strike the ball so
fierce.
Then came George Best, he
never liked to train –
He was always down the pub –
his drinking did remain.

Dennis Law came along – and
he also played for Man City,
Scoring a crafty goal – which
he really did so pity.
He was a Scot and he could
play – he was the prodigal son,
But that crafty little back-heel –
sent United to Division One!

Then came Sir Alex Ferguson –
he was a canny Scot,
He had all the best players in
sight – so he bought the blinking
lot!
He was so very successful, this
we can't deny,
But if he ever lost a game – he'd
give a little sigh!

He also conquered Europe, just
like the Busby babes,
Winning every trophy there –
and he never wore his shades!
His mouth would rotate a lot –
and more trophy's were to come,
Thanks to his winning style – and
his beloved chewing gum!!!!

Sir Alex has now retired – and Van
Gaal is now the manager –
Trying his best to win the games –
with Ryan Giggs, his deputy mentor.
They have been very busy – in
the signings of new players,
But missing out on a player –
that turned them all to jeers!!!!

We really love our football – that
is very clear,
Watching them run around – and
never show any fear!

The English Premier League – is
where the action is –
But don't forget the Champions
League – for it too is really BLISS!

FOOTBALL IS A GAME...
SIMPLY OUT OF THIS
WORLD

The planets float around all
day – within the outer space,
They sometimes chat and
watch TV – they do this so
with grace.
They've discovered a new
interest – which really does
intrigue,
They get together every
week – and watch the English
Football Premier League!

These planets have been so
dormant – but they discovered
a magic moment,
They were told of the English
Premier League – so they
checked out this installment!
They saw the angels all sat
down – watching Real Madrid –
They shouted and they clapped
their wings – just as all the
humans did!

Then the planets got a TV –
made by Panasonic,
They then started to watch
the football – and the teams
were really magic.

The planets were all so
amazed – and while watching
Barcelona –
When Barcelona scored a goal,
they shouted: 'HALLELUJHA!'

All the angels and the planets
had never seen this before,
They were watching European
football – 'oh, what a score!!!!'
The universe was all lit up –
as the planets lit up their lights,
And all the angels sat with
them – to watch the football
highlights!

They really were all cheering –
and the planets were so
excited,
'This game of earthling football –
is really very good – and we'll
have to watch Man United!
So every Saturday, they all
gathered round – like something
out of Star Trek;
'And watched all the European
football – the results they did
so check.'

These planets are also very
thrilled with the brilliant' Inter
Milan,
Watching them play in the
their space galaxy – everything

goes to plan.
The planets tell the angels – of
these fabulous new teams,
And when the magic floodlights
shine – you can see them in
your dreams.

From Saturn, Earth and Neptune,
and Mars soon follows suit,
Jupiter is also there – eating juicy
fruit!
The planets have now discovered –
a truly remarkable game,
From the European super teams –
all do make their name.

A new galaxy of planet stars – are
shining in the sky,
The planets are watching the football –
the English Premier League, so high.
The magic is all there – and the planets
are all so thrilled –
The super European football leagues –
their skill is now distilled.

The game of football and soccer, has
reached outer space,
The planets are so impressed – they
even do say grace!
When the games have ended – and
they meet their perfect hosts;
'The planets are now introduced – to
the brilliant O-Posts.'
So welcome to the game of football –

as the planets all shout; 'HOORAY!'
'Thank you so very much – and we'll
see you all on Saturday!!!!'

WELCOME TO WEST HAM...
UP THE HAMMERS

My name is Alf Garnett,
and I'm married to a
silly moo,
Every day I get up – she
tells me what to do!
I am a big West Ham
United fan – (up the
hammers!),
I follow them where-
ever they go – oh, I give
some lectures!!

I go to watch them play –
and I sometimes use
my wheelchair,
I ask Merrigold to push
me – because he's paid to care?
I do like to rant a lot –
and the West Ham shirt,
I will wear,
I can't control my
emotions – I always
have to swear!!

I also like the England –
when they won in 1966 –
Some say we were lucky –
some say it was a fix!!!!
I have my Sunday lunch,
and watch the TV soccer,
But, my irate wife is doing

the ironing – I really
should help her!!

But, I have to get ready –
to go and watch West Ham –
I get sick and very tired –
of travelling on a tram.
I have to make this
journey – ever single week,
Then I have to queue at
the match – they have a
bloody cheek!!

Once I am there – I sit in
the disabled area,
I keep a watchful eye out –
the stewards are always
there.
If I use my wheelchair –
and take Marigold, as well,
He's always prancing
around the place – he
really makes me yell!!

So, welcome to the
hammers – and West Ham
United,
You can all come in – but
only if your invited!!
Come and sit next to me –
and my carer – Marigold,
Enjoy the game – and
the win – well, this is what
I'm told!!!!

THOSE CLASSY PLAYERS...
WHO GRACE THE
ENGLISH PREMIER LEAGUE

We are the super football
clubs, and we play in the
English Premier League,
We are the elite of our
game – together, we do
intrigue.
We pride ourselves on
skill – for that there is no
doubt,
When we score a goal –
or two – the fans really
do shout.

We also entertain you –
as you do pay very good
money,
You sit in the stands in
the sun – also in pure
luxury.
We value you as our
supporters – that is very
true,
We will put on a super
game – especially for
you.

We run about all over
the pitch – we pass the
ball with ease,

With the fans all cheering –
we are just eager to please.
Families come and enjoy
the game – and children
all do cheer,
When half-time does arrive –
some adults enjoy a beer!

These teams are all
professional – they entertain
the fans,
Cheering, shouting and
dancing – it all happens in
the stands.
The atmosphere is superb,
and everyone is so happy,
Even a family sitting down –
they have a 'laughing' baby!

Saturday's are very special –
we love our football games,
Some of us go every week –
even naming all the names!
There is a shop you can go
to – to buy a football
programme,
Even a tasty sandwich –
tomato and some ham!

You can also buy a hot snack,
pie and peas is tasty,
Or a hot cheesy toasty – or
a delicious Cornish Pasty!
Hot drinks are also available –

to tempt your pallet more;
'From OXO, through to Bovril –
hot soup we all do adore.'

The fans come from
everywhere, just to watch
us play,
We always do entertain them,
in our own unique way.
The super stars are on display –
all of whom intrigue;
'Those classy, world class
players – who grace the
English Premier League.'

A WORLD CLASS PLAYER...
A PREMIER LEAGUE STAR

The Premier League, is
the league so great,
The stars come out –
with ball at feet,
Classy players, is what
they are,
Some will play a fine
guitar.

Running round the pitch
they do,
Never standing in any
queue,
Playing tricks with a
football now,
Now they go for their
chow.

They are first class – that
is true,
Playing for the privileged
few,
Sounds of; 'GOAL!' Come
to light,
It really is, a pure delight.

Please pass the ball to
me I ask?

I've got my lunch – and my flask,
Even now the team do play,
And some of us – will now pray.

Where's my shorts, they have got lost?
I need them now – I blame Jack Frost!
It's freezing cold – I'm not impressed,
The football game – is now addressed.

We are all united – that's for sure,
Winning more – we all adore.
Kissing is a joy to see,
Then come and sit – upon my knee!!!!

We are now ready, for the match,
The World Cup Final – where's the catch?
We're very proud – and glory be,
Now we play – on live TV.

All the teams are there
to see,
Entry now, for you is FREE.
The excitement grows,
here we go –
Come along to a soccer
show.

The world does watch,
as we all now play,
Hoping for a good display.
Italian players – and Spanish
too –
They're the best – of the
chosen few.

Come along and meet
your host,
The delightful team of
the O-Post.
Goal by goal – they will
bring you –
All the transfers – are
in the queue.

Settle down and rejoice
with me –
To watch the skills of
those you see,
The Premier League – is
the league,
Full of stars – and all
intrigue!

Here we go it's time
to play,
Watching now – it's a-okay.
Forever soccer – is what
we are,
A world class player –
a Premier League Star.

THE SKY SPORTS BLUES

Sky Sports now have
increased their prices,
All this and more – it's
no surprises,
Inflation leaps up to
the sky,
High prices – they can't
deny.

The Sky Sports team
know their football,
They commentate in
their own bubble.
Talking football – and
earning their pay,
All this and more – on
Saturday.

Jeff Stelling and friends,
they start new trends,
Reporting on games –
till the ends.
Former footballers –
do take part,
They're so very
passionate – right from
the heart.

Sky Sports do cover,
the Europe' too,

All this and more – just
for you.
Champions League – is
also there,
The World Cup hopes –
if we dare!

The Europe League's are
also great,
They are super skilled –
the fans create?
The FA Cup – Sky Sports
will cover,
I don't know why the
BBC do bother!!!!

The Sky Sports team still
sing the blues,
Cos no Premier League
team' likes to lose.
They chat and laugh at
each other,
The Sky Sports team…
the ball's in their quarter!

Just keep on watching
the Sky TV,
But you'll have to pay –
it isn't for free!
The Sky Sports Blues –
is what we all hear,
When a goal is scored –
there is a loud cheer!

So pull up a chair and
sit and cheer,
Eat some crisps – and
have a cold beer!!
The Sky Sports Blues
is the song to choose.
Because no Premier
League team likes to
lose!!!!

WELCOME TO OUR TEAM...
THE FIRST GAY MALE
FOOTBALLER

The football world is now
changing – something is
being revealed,
Something which will
make history – both on
and off the field.

For decades it has been
known – but no one dare
come out –
For fear of persecution –
and everyone would
shout?

The world of male football –
will change now, and for
ever,
True feelings are coming
out – we are now all
together.

"What am I talking about,
you ask me so politely?
The element of change,
my friends – for a whole
new sexuality."

The men's sport will now
feature – the first ever
gay man,
This will change the way
we play – accept it? Yes,
we can!

The first gay footballer –
is making history,
No more hiding away –
coming out to be free.

Welcome to the 21st
century – and we all
welcome this change
to be.
There's nothing wrong
with a gay footballer –
we welcome you with
glee.

The team accepts this
news – and smiles at
the star,
"Don't you worry, we
welcome you – now
you will go far."

More teams will follow
suit – as more players
come out as gay,

There's nothing to be
ashamed of – we love
you either way?

Everyone is happy – as
the gay footballer is now
here,
And when the full time
whistle blows – we can
enjoy a nice cold beer!!!!

All the bigotry is in the
past – and that is history,
For every footballer is
so equal – and that is
plain to see.

Hallelujha, I know this
now – and every man
is equal –
From footballers – to
the referee – the game
is now on schedule.

Everyone's the same –
no one is any different,
Now we play our football –
and enjoy the crowd
excitement.

Congratulations is for
sure – as barriers are
broke down.

From gay men – to
straight men – we all
wear one crown.

The world has now
made history – and
we salute it every year.
Please welcome to our
football team – the
'first gay football player

LOVE ME TENDER...
LOVE MY FOOTBALL

Love me tender, love
my football, tell me you
are mine,
For it's you that I do
love – and our hearts
entwine.
Love me tender, love
football – we are the
elite,
Welcome to the Premier
League, we don't
accept defeat.

Chorus:
Love me tender, we love
you – we mean that oh
so true,
For our O-Posts are
always there – we rely
on you.

Love me tender, I do
play, this is my home
league,
For you have been
good to me – creating
such intrigue.
Love me tender, love
football – we are the
champions –
For my darling I love

you – the darling soccer nations,

Chorus:
Love me tender, love our game, this is what we do,
For our darling football team – you are the special few.

Love me tender, love the sport, the light is shining bright.
We are playing at home today – we do feel such delight.
Love us tender, love the sport – for we can't always win,
For my darlings we will win – and this is not a sin!

Chorus:
Love my footy, love my team, you really are a dream.
For on the pitch you do deliver – and cause us all to scream.

Love me tender, love

the ref, for he is in
full charge.
He is always booking
us – for a foul of a
shoulder barge.
Love him tender, love
his style, the ref is
like a thistle,
When he retires from
the game – he'll blow
the final whistle.

Chorus:
Love me tender, love
football, the O-Posts
team are great.
They are up to date
for us – this we
appreciate.

Love me tender, I'm
in love – with the
skills of the modern
game.
All the players we
do see – but I do
not know their name.
Love me tender, love
football – it is a very
rich sport,
When you run out on
to the pitch – the ball
is in your court.

Chorus:
Love me tender, love
the dream – we really
are the host.
The world's best league's
are all on show, thanks
to our O-Posts.

Love me tender, we
love bath time, who's
now pinched the soap?
If we score some goals
today – we can all elope.
Love me tender, love us
true, this football we all
do play,
Never wondering why
we play – except for our
massive pay!

WE'RE FOOTBALL CRAZY...
WE'RE FOOTBALL MAD

Blue is the colour, Chelsea
is the team,
Then comes Everton – all
within a dream.
We're football crazy – we're
football mad,
And if our team do lose
again – we'll be so very
mad!

Red is the colour, Liverpool
are now mean,
Then comes the Arsenal,
somewhere in between!
We're football potty, we're
football loopy,
Welcome to Highbury, and
Anfield for your duty?

Winning is the order, losing
we do hate,
But every week we play our
game – it really is our fate.
Yellow is the colour, Leeds
are up there too,
So are Norwich City – those
canaries take their pew!

Then the half time whistle,
it blows now for half time,

We have to go to the shop –
and lots of stairs we climb!
Some people now are having
a drink – their throats are
very dry,
But that's not surprising –
when you're eating a nice
meat pie!!!!

Now it's back to the game –
but now I've lost my seat,
Someone has just scored a
goal – and I believe it was a
treat!!!!
I'm football crazy – I'm
football mad –
Now it is home time – I feel
so very sad.

Shouting as we go – and
waving our arms about,
Singing our beloved team –
to a rocking' twist and
shout!!!!
We also love our football –
and our dear old wives,
But only on a Saturday –
when they act like Dr
Phibes!!!!

Let's all sing together – as
footy is our dream,
Singing songs of football –
praising all the team.

Now we are so happy – now
to rest a while,
Let's all go to Blackpool Town –
and see the Golden Mile!!!!

THE BRILLIANT LIVERPOOL PLAYERS OF YESTERYEAR AND ANFIELD

We were the greatest Liverpool
team to ever grace the pitch,
We really were the kings of the
Kop – and all without a glitch.
We wore the red shirt of pride –
a very proud honour –
We always played majestically,
complimenting each other.

The Anfield team really were
supreme – we were feared by
all the rest.
Every match day on the Kop –
the fans – they were the best.
The cheers from the kop – was
unlike any other,
All the family's all did come –
and they all…'watched with
mother!'

The players too – they were
supreme – and they knew how
to pass the ball.
Tackling as they went along –
listening for the call?
Those awesome defenders –
protecting their goalkeeper,
Brilliant in their role – possibly

the saviour!

Kevin Keegan he was great,
he also played for England,
Emlyn Hughes had the blues,
they really are now legend.
Steve Heighway, he was there –
gliding down the wing,
Terry McDermott and Graham
Sounes – also did their thing.

They even had a 'super-sub'
who liked to call their bluff,
He always came on as a sub –
their saviour…David Fairclough.
Their goalkeeper was a gem –
he would always save them,
The ever reliable' Ray Clemence,
he jumped and dived in mayhem!!

One thing they had in common –
was their title' heir,
Also in the 70s – they all had curly
permed hair!
They played in all types of weather,
even in the snow.
They didn't wear woolen gloves –
real men you have to know!!

They really were the champions –
of Europe and the UK –
But unlike the boys today – they
didn't get very good pay!

They played for the love of the
game – that is very true,
And every Saturday at Anfield –
they played a game for you.

Kenny Dalglish was a player –
also a manager,
He came from Bonny Scotland –
he really was their saviour.
Joe Fagan was a sensation – a
manager, precisely.
Also in the same class – was
the brilliant Bob Paisley.

The managers of bygone years,
were all stars to know,
They all graced the Liverpool
shirt – their skills were all on
show.
But the legend of them all – a
brilliant man, honestly,
He commanded all respect –
the one and only…BILL SHANKLY.

The Liverpool team of the past –
like others – were a super team
to watch,
And every match-day in the bathtub –
they liked a drop of Scotch!!
The true greats of Liverpool – are
in our memory, far afield.
Welcome to the home of the
Liverpool…the brilliant ANFIELD.

THE MIGHTY LEEDS UNITED...
PLAYERS OF YESTERYEAR

Billy Bremner had a temper,
which was plain to see,
And if you tried to tackle
him – he'd kick you on your
knee!

There was also Peter Lorimar,
if he came at you, you'd
know it,
He also had a lethal right
foot – a shot just like a bullet!

Joe Jordan was a Scot, a fiery
one at that,
If you ever crossed him – his
fists would knock you flat!

There was even Jack Charlton –
and his brother, Bobby –
They both played for England,
alongside little' Nobby!

Then came Allan Clarke, a
quiet man, we gather,
He scored a winning FA Cup
goal – with a diving header.

Don Revie was the manager –

of the brilliant, Leeds United.
Now they are all in the past –
and some have now departed!

Leeds United, all in white –
were feared by most teams,
Trying their best to win the
game – if only in their dreams!

Now I end my journey – a
trip back in time,
A tribute to Leeds United
players, in a 'poetic' little rhyme.

THE AMAZING WORLD OF FOOTBALL TRANSFERS

The transfer news does
now amuse, big money
is paid on time,
Although many object –
is what we expect, it
really isn't a crime.

The agents are there –
and they do car, what
will the offer be?
A fee so big – you have
a jig – now you are
so free.

Sky Sports are there,
BT beware, to buy the
Premier League rights,
The highest bidder – is
the one that's quicker,
please, hold on to your
tights!!!!

The players are all world
class – vast fortunes
they all do amass,
They play so supreme, it
does seem a dream, they
really are sheer class.

Wheeling and dealings,
are seen as the trimmings,
the transfers are now on
the table,
So go with the flow, as you
all well know – the game is
now all stable.

With a dollar to spare, I
really do care – as I fly
across the Atlantic,
To see LA Galaxy, is my
own fantasy – it really
is pure magic.

Steven Gerrard is there, with
out any care, with Frank
Lampard – they now will go
far.
To play soccer in style,
they've waited a while –
in America – they are now
a big star.

The transfers are done – and
the football's begun, the stars
are set to do battle,
The Champions League – and
the English Premier League,
will now do battle as traditional.

CHELSEA SING THE BLUES...
WINNING GAMES IS WHAT
WE CHOOSE

We are the boys in blue,
and we are the ones to
trust,
When we march on to
the pitch – watching our
skill is a must.
We are the Chelsea elite,
we play at Stamford
Bridge,
And we are the defending
champions – because we
have the courage.

We won the Premier League,
in the summer of 2014,
Now we are defending it –
do you know what I mean?
We have a great defender,
the brilliant, John Terry,
We also had Frank Lampard –
but he went to Man City.

We have a wealthy owner,
and a flamboyant manager,
Known as the "SPECIAL"
one – he always hides his
anger!
Jose Mourinho is his name –
and he comes from Portugal,

Wanting to win ever game –
it is his football will!!

There even is Drogba, Ashley
Cole' as well,
Together as a strike force –
they really do so gel.
Lots of others too – all the
best right now,
When they parade on the
pitch – all the fans do bow.

The Chelsea boys are now
all ready – but, who do you
choose?
Even in the dressing room –
Chelsea sings the blues!!!!
So, good luck to the blues,
and Chelsea' is their name,
And winning the English
Premier League, is their
one true aim.

ARSENAL FOREVER...
WE ARE THE MIGHTY
ARSENAL

We are the mighty Arsenal –
we are a world-class team,
We play our game so
majestically, we really are
supreme.

We play in the English Premier
League – and we fear no
other team,
Not even Manchester United –
do you know what I mean?

Highbury is our home – we
also recruit beginners,
Our famous name is known
to all – we are the world-
class GUNNERS.

We really do have a history –
of famous players in time,
All were simply brilliant –
they really were sublime.

There was goalkeeper, Bob
Wilson – and the manager,
George Graham,
Every match they played –
it was a jam-packed stadium.

The most important game
they played in – was a classic'

FA Cup Final,
When Charlie George let
loose a shot – it really was
unstoppable.

But now they soldier on –
with a super manager,
And they continue to be
a world-class team, Arsenal –
forever.

THE ENGLISH PREMIER LEAGUE KICK-OFF

The Premier League has
now kicked off – we can
now applaud the players,
Walking on to the perfect
pitch – showing off their
kickers.
Boots all gleaming white –
and on occasions – shiny
yellow,
And if a footballer goes
up to the crowd – it's just
to say; 'HELLO?'

Out of the tunnel they
proudly march,
With their shirts and
shorts all ironed with
starch.
Fans all singing – as
they stand in a line –
All singing loudly – so
divine.

The referee is there –
looking so stern and
manly,
He has a pocket smart
phone – and listens to
Accrington Stanley!!
The referee's assistants –

stand and run the pitch,
All this and a lot more –
but sometimes there's a
glitch!!

The elite teams are all
in action – playing for
their lives,
Each player knowing –
only one survives!!
There can only be one
winner – or a score draw,
is an option,
When these top players
play – they really show
devotion.

So, welcome to the
home – of the English
Premier teams,
All of them knowing –
winning is their dreams.
So grab the remote
control – and settle down
to view,
The English Premier
League – is now here –
for me and for you!!

ENGLAND'S WORLD CUP MISERY

The World Cup Finals
we aim at – every four
long years,
But with the current
England team – it
always ends in tears!
No matter how we try –
or who the manager
is –
We always fail to
qualify – and we lose
on penalties!!

We used to be so
good – and we won
almost everything,
England's brave lion-
hearts – cannot win
anything!
Please excuse my
cynicism, I'd love to
be more positive –
But with the shabby
performances – of
the England's negative?

We seem to lack
the talent – and some
just don't qualify,
We never win anything –

it really makes us cry!!
England used to be –
the very best of all,
Walking out onto the
pitch – all feeling ten
foot tall!!

Even the European
Championships – we
never do any good,
And we have "world
class" players – as we
darn well should!!
We have got some
brilliant players – but
many are from over-
seas,
We don't have much
home-grown talent –
who can win for
England – with ease!!

And, why are they
always spitting? This
is so very dirty.
Running around
slobbering – getting
rather shirty!!
Maybe in the future –
England will reign
supreme,
Well, yes, I know, but
I can pray – if only in a
dream!!!!

WELCOME TO THE
CAPTIVATING WORLD
OF ENGLISH FOOTBALL

Welcome to the Premier
League – it is a world
away,
A league were all the
soccer players – get
very high pay.
The Arsenal, and the
Chelsea – Spurs and
West Ham –
Are all in the city of
London – near the
Birmingham!

Then there's Manchester
City – competing with
Manchester United,
These two play a mean
old game – and are now
so well divided.
Little Blackpool were in
a dream – and played the
top notch teams,
But, sadly, they got
relegated – the end of
all their dreams!

Fleetwood Town and
Accrington too – they
both played like silk,

Especially little Accrington –
by drinking plenty of
milk!!
Fleetwood will play
Blackpool – in Division
One –
Who will win this derby
match – and be the
prodigal son?

It isn't just about the
big boys – who are in
the top flight clubs,
But winning lots of
games you play –
depends on your good
subs!!!
The managers are there –
and they talk, shout
and scream,
Winning every game
they play – is their only
dream.

So, here we go again, to
a brand new soccer
season,
All the football clubs are
there – and all have very
good reason.
The Premier League, the
Championship – there's
Division One, too,
If any of them keep losing
games – they'll end up in Division Two!!!!

THE WORLD OF ENGLISH FOOTBALL AND USA SOCCER

The football season is now reborn,
The kissing of the players – is now the norm.
They score a goal – and scream like a woman –
They also dance – as their erotica is awoken!!

They run around on a pitch –
Stopping only – to wipe their snitch.
Over paid – and messing around,
In the dressing room – they pace the ground.

The world of soccer – in the USA –
All the boys all come out and play.
They have just signed David Beckham –
Followed by Steven Gerrard – a scouser'

they reckon!!

Diving they do – it's
now their culture,
Conning the ref – is
it any wonder?
But the kissing they
do – and it doesn't
look nice,
Are they behaving –
like they're running
a vice?

The English Premier
League, it is so very
rich,
Loads of talent – or,
is it a glitch?
Sky Sports and BT –
have paid over the
odds,
Raising my phone
line rental – the
greedy sods!!!!

Welcome to soccer –
in the USA –
Where everyone is
happy – come what
may!
So enjoy your football –
and feel the bliss;
'If you do score a goal –
do you have to kiss?'

THE RICE FIELDS OF THE PHILIPPINES

A land so far away, rich in love as we
pray,
The clear blue waters - wash the shore
as clean as the day.
The lovely green mountains are a God-
given delight,
Where the wind blows so pure, and
the sun shines so bright.

The heavenly villages are the home to
the people,
Who are so friendly – their love is
so ample.
The beaches too, are so clean and pure,
They lap up the sun – and the sea, which
we adore.

Behold! Those rice fields, they do look
stunning,
People sowing and people laughing,
The scenery, I love, and they smell so
good,
They were made by the people, with
some help from God!

The rice is precious, the Philippines so
lovely,
Children can go there, and admire the
beauty?
The rice is their life as it is from the lord,
The rice of the Philippines, I'd taste it, if I
could?

The fields stretch out for miles and miles,

Setting on green as the people all smile.
They cover the bed of flowers so true,
And sometimes there is – a love so true.

The rain does come and cleanse the
rice,
Which does make the rice taste so
nice?
Not just a harvest of income for thee,
The people work hard, and on their knee!

The sun and the moon both smile on
the rice,
The smile filled with love, and the love is
so nice.
The fields are the crown of luscious and
pure,
They are from God – as a present, I'm
sure?

The birds too, do fly up and over, to see
the rice and feel in clover?
They circle around in friendly song, taking
stock, as they love their master?
The master of trees, and the leaves so
green,
I know this for sure – but I've never been!

The Philippines, are beautiful, that's for
sure,
With love all around – we all do know?
The island so grand it warms your heart,
And you can feel the warmth, right from
the start.

So God bless the rice fields, you are so
loved,

You bless the Philippines, as only you could.
Go forth and grow, the rice which we love,
As our beautiful rice fields are sent from above.

We give thanks oh lord, for our lovely country,
We praise you too especially on Sunday.
Thank you for our fields of greenery' beauty,
We now do the harvest – as it is our duty.

THE GOOD LORD IS THERE

The good lord is there
he calls my name,
For thou art with me,
my heart feels so lame.
The holy path of thy
holy spirit —
Shall guide me home
as love I'll inherit.

I follow the scent of
the good lord, above —
Always thinking; 'will
I ever find my betrove?'
My heart is lifeless but
I feel no pain,
I carry on living — I
feel insane.

I must carry on and
seek thy love,
Maybe at times — I do
need a shove!
The darkness surrounds
me — I see no light,
I feel only sorrow — and
no delight.

I am now lost but I do
keep going,
To see the light — the
lord's homecoming.
The path of hope is so
hard to find —
I walk and I walk — but

still I am blind.
Nothing else matters,
I now shun this earth,
I'm going on a journey –
to a glorious rebirth.
Friend or foe, it now
means nothing –
Does god love me too –
or is he just bluffing?

I must carry on – I may
see the light,
I must find my sanctuary –
a special delight?
I follow my instincts – to
inhale a strength,
It must be there – I'm
not exempt!

Now I pray for a whole
new soul,
To free my mind from
this callous turmoil.
To find my way as I now
hear thy sounds,
The journey of my life –
it knows no bounds.

My mind is now free it
feels the fresh air,
The good lord has saved
me – because the good
lord is there.
My path I have now
found – I now face the
day,
To live my life freely –

because I do pray.

But, just as I was giving up — I felt a friendly hand,
Twas the hand of god — he said: 'I'll bless you where you stand.'
All of a sudden my deep depression had gone,
And I was given my life back — to truly be reborn.

So never fear the darkness, the light shall always shine through,
The good lord will always guide you — I know that to be true.
I will now face the day — and on Sunday I will pray,
I'll thank the lord for saving me — and ending my dismay.

I do now see the light — it shines so bright for me,
The good lord sends his love to me — and it is always free.
No more sorrow — no more sadness — just blessings all the way,
And as my heart beats happy again — it will

meet a brand new day.

*I now have a life and
the love of the lord,
I welcome new friends —
please, do come aboard?
I now see the light as I
now live with flair,
Knowing always; 'that
the good lord is there.'*

THE GOLDEN RAINBOW

The rainbow climbs through
the sky,
With a pot of gold somewhere
up high.
How does one reach this true
gift?
When the blue sky above –
attend their annual shift?

They do keep guard over this
gold,
But I'd like to share this, with
the poor and the old.
May I borrow the gold from
the rainbow?
I promise you friends – no one
else will know!

It will be our secret, like the
rainbow itself,
Never to know just what is
wealth.
The rainbow now I must climb,
But never a true word, spoke
in rhyme!

So with my spirit I now depart,
Upon the journey to find the
heart.
The heart that holds the mystery
on
How the rainbow keeps it's golden
run?

THE GLARE OF THE CANDLE

Beware the glare of the candle
For it is known to man-handle
Any one who takes a peep
As it will attack your soul to keep?

You attempt to light it but it isn't
responding
It seems to have life as a spooky offering.
But be very aware of the piercing glare
For it is in some way aware.

You can look at the candle in peril
But your mind will be sent to the devil
How do you tackle such an evil flame?
That lights up the room in shame?

It does have the power to assist
The dead who awake from their rest
The glare of the candle is evil
And will shake your mind to its peril?

You can look at the flame of the candle
But what you may see is evil
Don't be afraid it's only a flame
But the shame is the name of the game?

Now I must go and see the flame
That looks so plain and has a name
The name is Dare – so if I can handle
Will I look at The Glare of The Candle?

THE GENIUS OF WILLIAM SHAKESPEARE.

I am the Bard of words
and all,
When I stand to attention -
I feel so tall.
What's my name - I
hear you inquire?
Nobody special - just
William Shakespeare!

I was born before my
time, the ladder I did
climb.
I started to write my
trustee old rhyme.
Armed with a flexible,
and bendy quill,
But I kept on drinking -
my hands never still.

Dreaming up words
and writing them down,
Sometimes this writing
did get me down.
Armed with my mug of
tea and toast,
I used to be known as
the perfect host.

I wish I'd been born
in the future in time.
And getting to grips
with a computer in
mime.
Maybe an Iphone - a

laptop and more.
Clicking and pressing -
oh, what a bore!

My friend Mr Poe, a
writer of horror.
I'll meet him in person -
sometime tomorrow.
Hamlet and Mr Usher,
with the old pendulum.
All this dramatics - it
sounds like bedlam.

I may have embraced
this Google in time.
Embracing the computer,
I'd write perfect rhyme.
I am on stage with my
quill at my side.
The ideas in my head -
they so want to hide.

I am a playwright - I
write for pleasure.
But something tells me
I'll be known for ever.
Just like my friend -
who often felt low.
A writer of horror -
Edgar Allan Poe.

We both used
candlelight on an old
wooden table.
The candle did flicker -
our hands now stable.
We write all through

the night, taking a
drink,
We both needed a
tonic - it helps us to
think.

But I myself am called
a Bard,
I know not why - Mr Poe's
in the yard.
We talk about horror -
and about short poems.
Trying to make more
golden rich coins.
Who would have thought
that we'd live forever.
Our writings world
famous - that's our
endeavour.

It's just a shame we
were in different times.
We could work together -
we'd have written perfect
rhymes.
My death was long ago
and it certainly brought
tears,
William Shakespeare -
happy 400 years!
Read the book my friends,
and look at it hard.
I wrote that book - I'm
known as the Bard.

The passing of time has
resurrected my soul.

I hear the parades, I do
hear them call.
For 400 years my soul
lays still.
But I now write in Heaven,
at my own free will.
The passing of time -
and maybe a tear,
You'll always remember
me...William Shakespeare.

HAPPY 400th ANNIVERSARY TO WILLIAM SHAKESPEARE

My name is William Shakespeare,
and I don't get all this fuss.
So I am 400-years-old, but I still
need to travel by bus!
The BBC are going overboard,
to mark my special day.
But if you are like me - I feel so
much dismay!

Yes, it is true, I wrote poems all
day long.
Only breaking to eat my food -
when I heard the dinner gong.
I don't class myself as special -
in any shape or form.
But my writings are classed as
classics - and really cause a
storm.

I also write my poems - but they
aren't very good.
I really could do a whole lot
better - yes, I know I should.
The world has marked my special
day - though I don't know why;
'Every time I read a play - it really
makes me cry!'

I don't really like my poems - they're
boring to a tee.
Yes, you can pay for a book -
they're not for "BLOODY FREE!"
There are lots of other famous

writers - and who are old just like
me.
But the BBC never mentions them -
it's plain enough to see.

I didn't use a computer - or a type
writer - just a bleeding wobbly
quill,
I also suffered from writer's cramp -
and had to take a pill!
I got no joy out of writing - but its
what I did all day.
Dipping my droopy quill in the ink -
and spilling ink in my tray!

I really had a vision - and I saw a
computer aloft.
I never thought that 400 years on -
we'd be writing with Microsoft!
But even in my own despair, I heard
the sound of a bugle.
Sounding the arrival of the computer
and the geeky GOOGLE!!!!

But I did it all myself you see - writing
every day and night.
But I just didn't realise - my works
would be such a delight!
Happy 400th anniversary - and may
my writings make you all cheer.
Thank you one and all - from a very
old...WILLIAM SHAKESPEARE.

THE GENIE

He lurks in his world
inside his palatial bottle,
But sometime's he gets
fed up – and wants to
pull full throttle!
He can be quite miserable,
that is a fact,
But when someone
strokes his bottle, he pops
out and uses tact!

In the days gone by, he
had very special powers –
And he would grant you
all a wish – while watching
Fawlty Towers!
This genie hated MPs,
as I do, we both did agree,
As they all get their freebie
bills – everything is
free.

They had to go and we
planned a plan,
But the genie up and
ran!
But I soon gave chase
bottle in hand –
But I got caught sinking
in the sand.

"I will destroy this English
government – I will make
England great,

So off we went to make our
history – oh it'll be a treat!
The genie and I both sat
round the fire – our plan we
did admire,
Planning our massacre of all
MPs, now I am a Sire!
"But first we have to eat –
and oh, the last supper?
With a drink of wine and a
beer, our actions just might
suffer?"
"We need a clear head – for
what we are to do –
To rid this England of MPs –
and then dash off to the loo!

THE GUNPOWDER PLOT

Sitting in the cellars of
the eerie Parliament
building,
All my thoughts are so
baffled – picturing them
all burning.

I stroke my little combed
moustache, and think of
my dastardly plot,
While planning my escape –
and living on my yacht.

The stinking cellars of
parliament, would soon
be cleansed in blood,
And all those grasping
royals – and MPs – will
soon die like I know they
should.

My eyes are dark but
shine so bright – glancing
at the fuse,
Ready and willing to light
it – goodness, it does
amuse!

I hear them shouting in
the halls – as the terror,
I hear their calls.
All of them will soon be
history – my name will
run the course.

I sit on my barrel – and
take a puff – of my proud
havana cigar –
And just before I light the
fuse – I hear a fine guitar!

The light is bare – but I
don't care –
I sit here charming – in my
lair.
My colleagues are waiting
for my escape – I will now
light the fuse;
'But, oh my god, I hear
footsteps dashing down-
oh why does that not amuse?'

I sit so calmly with my hands
so black – I shake my soul,
to wake,
Those insidious parasites
I will destroy, and feel the
building shake!

Just then the door is burst
open – armed guards stand
there so stern,
Have I failed in my plot – the
parliament to burn?

'My attempt is dashed and I
am seized, now my plan will
rot,'
'But please do remember my
good intentions – 'the dastardly,
gunpowder plot!'

THE HOMELESS.

The homeless are not
aliens - they are human,
just like us all,
Its just they've had
some bad luck - and
on hard times they
do fall.

They scour the streets
of the land,
Hoping a kind stranger
will give them a helping
hand,
They lay in the cold of
winter - inside their
cardboard box,
And if they catch a chill -
they might catch chicken
pox!

We see this problem
every day - and it really
shouldn't happen,
When mankind fails to
act - loneliness will ripen.
To be cast aside like a doll,
and to be jeered at every
day,
When all the homeless
really want - is to feel
a-okay!

This is a serious problem -
and especially now,

We must find a way to stop this - provide some shelter, somehow.
Roaming the streets isn't the answer - and not in this day and age,
And when the local authorities ignore it - it puts me in a rage!

We could provide more centres - and food and drink to share,
And a friendly chatter - before this is so rare?
Just to listen - and to smile - this could prove a lifesaver,
Then if you can afford it - donate a nice new dollar!

This happens all over - even in poor countries too,
It is poverty - and children suffer, I tell you this is true.
People in high places who live in posh big houses,
They don't know the real truth - they can't see past their own noses!

Welfare is partly to blame - with the poor losing their welfare
If they are disabled - they'll

lose all - and that's not
fair.
They target the disabled -
and the vulnerable of society,
It isn't right, I tell you - they
need help - and on occasions
pity?

Food banks are now popular
all over the land we see,
They provide food and advice -
for you and for me.
The rich just get richer - and
the poor are left to rot,
And as the single mother - lays
her baby in a broken cot.

The world would be a better
place - if poverty wasn't here,
But there's nothing we can
do about it - but try to bring
good cheer.
A simple smile, a simple wave,
this really would be better,
And if more people spoke to
each other - things would
improve forever.

But this is not an ideal world -
and there are a lot of sinners,
But they can be reformed - and
be the new beginners!
The homeless could be a thing
of the past - and this I so do
pray;
"Especially at times like this -
some warmth on Christmas Day."

So, please, spare a thought -
and if you can a smile,
And watch the face light up -
instead of going on trial!
This is my prediction - to end
all poverty -
But I can't do it alone - I need
help, seriously!

From government leaders -
to council sinners - their help
is what we need,
And maybe one fine day - we
will all say; 'they did a very
good deed.'
So embrace your life as never
before - and say; 'thank you
for your warm home,'
Because if you weren't so
lucky - the streets you may
just roam?

THE HOMELESS...PART TWO.

The homeless do need
help - not condemnation
every day,
We should help them
more - in our own way.
A smile and a chat - or
a cup of tea to give,
And maybe a sandwich -
we all should forgive.

It happens every day -
and they feel such
dismay,
The homeless are all
human - this is true
today?
Walking the streets
they do - often feeling
low,
But we can make a
little difference - and
good cheer is good to
know.

The homeless just
want a home - just like
you and me;
'They're even willing to
pay for it - in rent for
all to see?'
The bedroom tax doesn't
help them - nor the local
authorities;
If they help the homeless

to get a home - they're
hit by a sanctions swizz!!

The homeless want to
work - and pay taxes like
all other people -
They don't want any hand-
outs - this is pure and
simple.
The welfare advisers
are like computers -
"Next person, please? It's
all electronic disorders?"

The homeless wander
from place to place -
Just trying to get a grip
on the human race?
In cold weather they
will freeze -
In warm weather - they
feel at ease!
But, being homeless isn't
nice - and no one should
live like this -
If only with a little help -
their life could be so bliss!

A hot bath - and a good
hot meal, can perk your
spirits high,
And when you're out of
the rain - your clothes will
feel so dry?
A little compassion - and
a will to care -
To eradicate this homeless

problem - we do it because
we dare?

We can all help solve this
problem - that is so very
true -
If you see a homeless
person - say; 'hello, - how
are you?'
Give a little blessing - and
see their face light up with
glee,
And you will see with your
own eyes - being friendly is
so FREE!

So my new year message
to the government, is to try
to help the poor -
Give them all some hope -
don't rob their benefits
even more?
Make 2015 a happy year -
and try and spread good
cheer,
But just from me - and the
lord - I wish you all; A
Happy New Year.

THE LAND OF LOVE...
THE HEAVENLY PHILIPPINES.

The land of love
is so far away,
It is so beautiful -
come what may.
Lush green hills -
and clear blue
sea,
Just for you -
and of course,
for me.

The sea is blue
and washes the
shore,
It's warmed by
the sun - a
heavenly cure.
The beach is fine
and soft as silk,
All this and more -
as I drink my milk.

A magic land of
love and dreams,
May I present the
beautiful Philippines.
A heavenly place
of love so sweet,
I long to go there -
for a treat.

True love is there -
that is so true,

My honey is there -
my love for you.
God bless this land
in your dreams,
The beautiful culture -
of the heavenly
Philippines.

THE LITTLE ANGEL OF BAGHDAD

She was four years old was Angel
She lived in Old Baghdad.
Her home was a tiny hovel
With her mum and dad.

Her mother called her Angel
She had that kind of grace,
Beautiful and smiling
So angelic was her face.

Like little girls all over,
In spite of poverty,
Her laughter could get out of hand
So full of girlish glee.

Her present on her fourth
birthday
The joy showed in her eyes,
A little doll made of rags
It was a big surprise.

The doll meant all the world to her
It was a real delight.
Wherever she went it went
too
It never left her sight.

The other night a smart bomb
While Angel dreamt her dreams
Hit her little hovel
Smashed it to smithereens.

Now smart bombs are expensive
A million pounds some cost.

But this one wasn't very smart
It got completely lost.

They buried Angel of Baghdad
As thousands stood and cried,
And the rag doll that she loved so much,
Was right there by her side.

So if you're there St Peter,
Please prepare these things,
A halo for a four year old
And a little pair of wings.

P.S. So it's the same old story
Since the world began
The slaughter of the innocents
Man's humanity to man.

War seems normal to the elite
And sadly, with no end in sight.
Until the pen-pushers in their office
Start to end all wars, they promise?

God bless you little Angel,
For in heaven you will mingle.
The heaven you have found,
Is now safer than the ground.

So sad is this, my story true,
But shed no tear Angel asks of you?
Angel smiles and plays so happy now,
As we all take our final bow.

THE PAIN OF DEMENTIA

In time we all get older,
and we may feel so
lost,
Our bones grow weaker
by the day - as they
are attacked by evil
Jack Frost.
We try to keep our
sanity - and our minds
do wander away,
Making all our loved
ones - feel in total
dismay.

Our world can seem
unimportant - as our
memory slowly dies,
And we can no longer
see the sun - or the
beautiful blue skies.
All our thoughts are
terminated - as we
lose the will to live,
But before god does
call us - we all need
to forgive.

Dementia is a killer -
and it destroys our
bodies and our souls,
And all I want to do -
is see the water falls?
We lose the will to
live and more - and

life is not the same,
This dementia has
taken over - and now,
I know not my name.

Depression and mental
health - are also on
the rise,
We cannot see it coming -
even with two good eyes!
It creeps upon us slowly -
and you know it will
succeed,
It really does tear your soul
apart - it also makes you
bleed.

Upon this earth we are
put - but nothing is
guaranteed -
Perhaps our loving families,
can argue their evil greed?
Dementia is so evil - yet
there is no known cure,
But with the help of God,
our king - he will help us -
this I'm sure!!

Forgive those who trespass,
and make our lives so bitter,
Pray for their little souls -
and they too might get
better!!
So never fear as we all live
once - and shed a little
tear,
And one day in the future -

dementia, we will not fear.

Lift up the soul you have
to hand - and feel the
gift of life;
'And as we age - our hearts
will grow older - and never
know any strife.'
Bless us all I ask this now -
as we live to love an idea,
And never again - upon
this earth - will we suffer
the pain of DEMENTIA.

THE RIVER OF LIQUID GOLD

The river of no return
It is sacred, and in we
learn.
The river will cleanse
the soul within,
As you feel life, will
just begin?

Just take a taste of
the river of dreams,
It can only feel good,
as you hold the beams?
The beams of love flow
through the river,
Always looking - as you
swim ever nearer?

Just go with the flow,
as the river takes you,
From the shore to the
middle - you'll be there
too?
Just like magic - you find
you can swim,
A miracle, indeed, it is
a sweet dream?

You will return via the
river,
Never say no, never say
never?
The river has cleansed
the world of evil,
Never again - will we

fear the devil?

Gold has been found in
the river of dreams,
Now we can all share
in our dreams, supreme?
Liquid gold, does lighten the
way,
Is all we need - as it is all
okay!

Just take a tour of the river
so pure,
It really refreshes - just like
the shore?
Enjoy the water and all that
is good,
As the lord has made it -
like he should.

*The river of Gold, is pure
in itself,
It will surprise you - and I
know that well.
The golden fleece is now
discovered,
Or is the magic - the lord
has uncovered?*

THE SANDS OF TIME

The sands of time are very dry
But the lord looks down and
quenches thy sty.
To bleach the sand in the far
away land,
Only the blessed can take the
hand.

The sand is dry and not so good
As the thirst in you dies, as the
God.
To trek through this land will be
insane,
You'll get through – but in great
pain.

The sands of time are told to us,
From the Gods right above thus
Behold, the land which drinks the
sand,
Served from the lord – from his hand.

We live and breathe the sands
of time,
With the lord's help – it can be
divine.
The mythical magic of the sands
of time,
May progress now – in all the shrine.

The land we know, does tell the time,
For us all to live in the midst of entwine.
God Bless the land with harvest chime,
And God Bless us – in the sands of time!

THE SANITY OF MY MIND

The ghosts in my mind,
are all feeling the pain,
As the devils of darkness
do battle to slain.
The wretched demons
that plague my soul,
They all do battle with
a demonic call.

I must carry on and live
for today;
'But so far today – all I
feel is dismay.'
A mysterious visitor
invades my mind,
As their insidious
behaviour makes my
mind blind.

I dress very smart as
an act I do show,
But deep in my soul –
I always feel low.
I wear shiny shoes to
guide my feet –
They guide me home
in sour defeat.

People do look at me
in surprise,
They ogle my suntan –
which meets their eyes.
Compliments they deliver
as I stand alone –

*Why do I feel like, I'm
dead on my own?
I grasp at the shock of
the compliments I do
hear,
But why do I feel I am
in fear?
To be loved is my aim
that's all I want,
Maybe I'll find love as
I drink from the font.*

*To live alone is all well
and good —
Having no one to talk to —
I do feel like mud.
Love is a gift which I
seem to have lost,
And my love life is none —
just like Jack Frost.*

*I feel rejected like a
person who's ill,
No one cares — I feel
over the hill.
The act I portray is of
a happy person —
Just give me an Oscar,
to compliment a
perversion?*

*To enhance the love
of a God-fearing woman,
Is all I do want — now, I
have spoken.
Mistakes I've made I kid
you not —*

*But at this moment my
life is a tied knot,*

*I see the light at the
ahead in a daze,
Is this for real? Or, am
I now to feel craze?
I urge my soul to
enhance my thoughts,
I need to find my
sanctuary – as my soul
now floats.*

*The sun I now see – it
warms up my soul,
The fear is dispersed –
I now hear the call.
My heart beat is now
steady – that does feel
good,
I see my life changing –
as it now should.*

*I aim to move forward
and enhance the fresh
air,
I do this with confidence,
because I now dare.
I feel I've won the battle
and the war –
As I now walk with more
confidence – I could even
go far!*

*The highway is now
brighter — as I feel the
love of God,
The sanctuary of eternal
life — is as it is; I nod.
To always believe in my
self — will always be my
aim —
And all my depression
will evaporate — just like
the eternal flame.*

*I am now free of the pain
which invaded my tortured
soul,
No more panic and being
afraid of the invading troll.
For love and happiness
shall bless my days in kind;
'And never again to fear —
the sanity of my mind.*

THE SINISTER LAMP

There was a lamp that was rather sinister
You just didn't know if it was glaring at you
The lamp did seem to have a life force of true
And those who looked on were soon sent to drool

Their life would change and so it was seen
This lamp could hold you in a tight dream
Things would change for the beholder
Too many glares and you would turn colder

Was this lamp evil or was it a saviour?
Pick it up - I dare you dear listener?
Just hold the lamp up and glare at your peril
Just one look may drive you to the devil

Don't show your friends as they will turn
Into something and you're stomach will churn?
Please be aware of the nastiness inside
This monstrous lamp which can drive you mad?

For it is said good will follow
Are you tempted to see tomorrow?
With your friend in mind you weep
But inside the lamp – I dare you to peep?

We may if we're lucky, see through this spirit
That hides away and possesses your merit
Turn the lamp off and expel it to the loft
Will you do it? Go on, don't be soft?

Now the lamp's gone and we see the light
Of the sun and the moon as they shine so bright
Has the lamp gone – you seem to have cramp?
The spirit that lives - in the glare of The Lamp!

THE WONDROUS PHILIPPINES

The lord smiles down on the
islands we know,
Where fruit and flowers all
do grow,
The sea is blue – and is so clear,
You can take a swim – or a
paddle with your darling, so
near?

The sky is so blue, as blue
as the sky,
It looks so amazing – that
we can't deny.
The birds do sing – as the
morning wakes
You can see those wondrous
clear blue lakes?

Vegetation is lush – as green
as the grass,
As the animals feed in the
green fields, alas!
The beautiful bounty does
spread her charm,
But no one there – comes to
any harm.

The people are so friendly –
and beautiful too,
They live quietly – and hardly
ever argue!
The markets are busy – and
sell everything you require,
Their love for each other – is

a real treasure.

The love of the islands, are
plain to see,
They smile with beauty, just
for thee?
Come on and visit, the charm
is so neat,
They really are a perfect treat.

Flower girls are there – as
stunning as the flower,
Their beauty holds the secret –
and the power?
The air is filled with love –
which is blessed from the
above.
God's love is shown – as the
land shares its trove.

There is no other beauty, as
the Philippines so true,
The beauty we call for another
love for you?
Listen to the flowers, they sing
in the fields,
Together in harmony – as true
love does flourish and steals?

The wondrous Philippines are
a beauty to behold,
They share their love and their
story is told.
Bless them all – I say that so
true,
The wondrous Philippines – we
do all love you.

THE WINDOW

You sit by the window day and night,
You watch all the life as it appears so bright?
The window of hope is a watchful sign,
Just stare all the way - and time will be mine.

The visions you'll get are just like images,
So colourful to as they create the barges.
Waiting for you to explore even more,
Just like the vision shown through the door?

You gaze through the window at life we know,
But it does seem so slow as fast we grow?
Does this mean life as we know it well,
Just look through the window – we do dwell?

The window is magic like a planet of joy,
You may even see the sweet girl and boy?
The wondrous sights are given to you,
Just by viewing the window so true?

But life through the window can also be bad,
Just don't open it up as the magic is sad?
The window looks at you right glaringly back,
Don't worry, my dears, it's your shadowy rack?

But when do we know when our window is happy?
It shows all the good folk all happy as Larry?
Let us look further and what do we see?
A life so wondrous - like a wave on the sea?

So look at the window and look at it good,
You'll see lots more as you know you should?
Please take your time and look really well,
As the lords face does stare as we do dwell?

TO BREAK YOUR LOVERS HEART

You stand there feeling numb,
and you can't think what is
wrong,
You feel so hurtful inside your
soul – you just want to bang
on the gong.
Your love heart is no more –
and you didn't know the score,
They just up and left you – they
just showed you the door!

What has gone so wrong, you ask
yourself?
You feel so bad – like you fell off
the shelf!
Where has she gone to - you really
want to know?
As deep in your soul – you really
feel so low.

Nothing else matters – as you
feel in tatters –
In secret you mourn – and spill
the tears.
Why has she gone and left you
alone?
All you want is your home sweet
home.

Your heart feels empty – as you
break inside,
All you want to do – is float with
the tide.
My heart is broken – now I'm no

more,
Where do I go? Through death's dark door?

No more this pain I will endure,
I now do leave you – that's for sure.
To another new land – which looks so very grand –
And with the angels I will walk – maybe hand in hand!

Adios my friends as the light is now turned out.
For the final journey – that I'm in no doubt.
To be at peace is all I want to be, out of this earth I go –
And no more hurt will I ever feel – never again will I feel so low.

The peace of heaven is all I feel, and the bliss is there for me,
A place of tranquil and of love – is where I want to be.
No more pain or broken hearts – that is a guarantee,
And if my soul does feel sad – I'll just have a cup of tea!

I feel the silence of the heaven – and the comfort of the holy spirit,
My destiny is now all here – my heaven is what I inherit.
So no more hurt from my heart –

who went without a word,
The way she went – and nothing
was said - it really is absurd!

PLEASE FALL IN LOVE WITH ME

When you feel rather
down - you feel so bad
inside,
You just don't feel like
socialising – all you do
is hide.

But believe in God – as
your saviour – and you
will never doubt,
And you will walk that
angel path – and feel
the need to shout?

The Holy Ghost is there
for you – his love will
shine so bright,
Then you will face the
day ahead – and feel a
great delight.

The angels are playing
their tunes of love – as
they fly around so free –
And then you will feel a
special power – it's true
love sent from me?

The lord is my shepherd –
my light – my soul – as
my life now sees the
light;
'And now I'll walk in the
path of the lord – I only

know it's right.'
The paradise of happiness,
is there – and it is free,
Just take a step to find the
lord – it may be under the
tree!

The guidance you seek – is
given to all – as the sheep
flocks to the barn,
And the light will shine
within your heart – as you
welcome a whole new morn.

Just believe and you shall
seek – the way to happiness –
As the good lord hears our
cries for help – our souls he
will so bless.

The hurt you feel within
your heart – will now all
disappear –
And because you're free of
eternal pain – you may just
shed a tear.

Take hold of the love which
is given to you – and it will
pierce your heart;
'And love and happiness
shall be yours – and a loving,
brand new start.'

Take my hand, oh precious
lord – I feel your love and
more –

To live with love – and no
pain or grief – I really will
adore.
The love of the shepherd –
shines in his sheep – and
the sun will shine on thee,
Won't some kind lady
hear my plea; 'and fall in
love with me?'

BEATING DEPRESSION

Sitting here in my chair
I just gaze outside – and
just stare.
I watch the world go
silently by,
I'd like to be there – as
I do cry.

My torment is in my soul,
and it is spreading,
I have to be punished –
but is this my ending?
I refuse to be beaten –
and I will fight my cause,
Because somewhere in
the future – I will fight,
I knows?

The tablets do help me –
they calm me down –
If I don't take them – my
brain would drown!
I look into the light – as
my soul feels so right –
This has to be the way –
the light is so bright?

No one can see how I
feel inside –
That's why most days
I do try to hide.
My inner self is what
I do feel,

I just want to get better –
and feel so real?

This hidden illness is not
so visible,
So people condemn you –
and it makes you feel ill.
They are so judgemental –
and also offensive -
They seem to look through
you – and see the negative?

Dear Lord, above, please
hear me now;
'Help me get through this –
I need hope, somehow?'
I know I can beat this
feeling, I suffer,
To be set free – while my
life takes a stutter.

I know with help I can
combat this illness –
All I feel is sadness – I
do feel a mess.
Please show me the way –
there must be a reason:
"Help me to beat my
horrible depression?"

I'm in your hands, I now
accept ,
I have sleepless nights –
I haven't yet slept.
To wake from my dream,
and feel so free,
To beat this depression –

I do ask of thee?

To summon the life that
was born unto me,
To hold your hand – and
smile with glee.
To go to places without
any fear,
Depression, be gone – I
so want to cheer?

I look at the sun in the
clear blue sky –
Oh, my goodness – I so
want to fly.
The world looks different –
and feels a pleasure,
No more depression – it
has gone forever.

You see, this dreadful
illness you cannot see,
But I'm not a monster –
I live by the sea.
To walk on air – and sing
out loud,
I beat depression – now
I love the crowd.

I say this to you – who may
suffer like me;
'Never give up – and you
will be free.'
Just pray to God as your now
in remission –
And, trust in God – as you

beat your depression.

BEATING MY DEPRESSION

I sit here and I wish away,
At the same time – I feel dismay,
No feeling I have - and no emotion I show,
The clock ticks away – and it is painfully slow.

The world goes on – I see that so clearly,
I used to love life – I mean that so dearly.
Now it doesn't matter as it isn't the same –
A horrible illness - makes me feel insane.

I try to fight this illness, I've unfortunately got,
It wrecks my brain – to total rot.
The life is sucked from out of my soul,
I daren't go out – in case I feel small.

I try to look smart – that is the key,
But no one can see my enemy in me?
I always get compliments – that is good –
But why does this not improve my inner-self mood?

The whole world around me
seems to close in –
And I consider having a gin!
But this will not make me
feel any better –
The inner person inside me -
it just takes shelter.

People will stare – and people
will think –
They'll also judge you – before
you can blink!
What the heck – you must stay
calm,
You may need a friend – to hold
on to your arm?

Guidance, and tolerance – is the
name of the game,
So why aren't we treated just
the same?
Someone to listen – and someone
to care,
Before I crack up – and jump
through the air!

What makes me so sad? What
has gone wrong?
Why do I hear a horrible gong?
To be free of this menace – and
suffer no more,
Just to be happy – is what I adore.

Just to be free from this horrible
illness –
And then to find happiness – and

maybe forgiveness?
Where do I go? Where do I search?
Is the answer, my, friends,
somewhere in church?

In God's holy house – that's were
I'll look,
Under the seats – but I feel like a
crook!
Tablets I take – they help me to
cope –
What are my options – to hang by
a rope?

What is the cause? Is there any
pause?
I want to get dressed – in my best
clothes?
People still laugh – but I do not
care –
I now feel good – and so does my
hair.

This illness, I'm winning, and take
each day as it comes,
I now feel better – no more aching
bones!
Life has new meaning – I have a
new mission –
This illness I had – it is known as;
DEPRESSION!!!!

CREMATION

My time on earth is now
at an end,
I'm going to a better place –
to start a whole new trend.
I see a flame which shines
all around,
The warmth I feel is music
in sound.

I lay down in peace, to be
resurrected,
My body lies in comfort –
spiritually protected.
I had to decide on burial
or cremation –
The one I choose – will
be my holy salvation.

I am peacefully sleeping,
as I pass into the flames,
Cremation of my life –
but my soul still remains.
I feel no more pain but
the flames feel surreal,
I now enter heaven – a
new life to reveal.

I meet the boss as he
welcomes me home,
The angels are singing –
I see Elvis on his throne.
We chat together as God
speaks to the nation;
'Burial or Cremation?

which will be your...
Final Destination?'

GOD DEFEATS THE TYPHOON

An island so far away
is beaten by a tyhoon,
People have to evacuate
before night – and high
noon.

The beaches are now
deserted – the sand
blows upon the shore,
The sea is a raging wall –
but God knows the
cure.

The sea tries to come
ashore - but it fails as
God does protect –
His mighty hand he
raises high – he does
not neglect.

The wind does howl –
but God stamps it
quiet –
He will not tolerate –
he helps the people
to evacuate.

The air is harsh, as
the rain lashes down,
But God stands up –
in his gown.
"Stay back, I tell you –
fear me you will –
And he threw the

typhoon off the hill!"
He raises his almighty
hand – and demands
the storm's retreat,
He says; "No one will
hurt my people – I
insist you accept
defeat."

So God protects his
loyal people – he
loves them all you
see,
He even punches
the typhoon – and
the people are now
free.

IF TOMORROW BRINGS LOVE

If tomorrow hails a brand
new day,
I'll always love you in my
way.
The sun shall shine in my
heart,
And our love together
shall never part.

If tomorrow seems so far
away,
My love for you will never
stray.
My heart beats lovingly
like a beat,
My love for you – it beats
a treat.

If tomorrow seems a bit
too much,
I'll hold your hand – you'll
love as such.
Tomorrow is full of a loving
smile,
For your love – I'll swim
the Nile.

If tomorrow brings a new
love for us,
We both can love – while
on the bus.
Tomorrow will shine for
me and you,
My love for you – is all so

true.
Tomorrow shall hail a
brand new beginning –
No more sorrow – no
more pining.
I'll love you more every
new day,
This is my pledge – I've
now found our way.

You are my life – without
any strife,
We are as one – as man
and wife.
Our love did blossom for
tomorrow to bless,
The sun shines down
as our special new guest.

If tomorrow brings love –
and happiness to me,
It means you're sat comfy
upon my knee.
Tomorrow's blessings –
make's our love so rare,
I'll love you always – my
heart, to swear.

If tomorrow is blessed with
a bride and groom –
Please love my heart –
there's plenty of room?
If tomorrow starts and
ends my heart,
I'll know forever we found
love from the start.

Love me my honey – for I
long for your touch,
Let's switch off the lights –
and use a torch?
Our love was blessed as
a gift from above;
'Our prayers will be
answered – if tomorrow
brings love.'

MY HAUNTED MIND

The haunted mind is invading us,
So what do we do to lift this curse?
The army of the darkness is sinfully here,
I now face pain – and shed a tear?

The curse of the mind is plain to see,
When the evil of mankind, is as blind to me?
Help me, please, I make this plea,
Even if I go down on bended knee?

Satan is devlish – he is around,
You don't see him – he makes no sound!
Come to thy god, is what I ask,
When we can drink – from the refreshing flask?

The mind is in trouble, mental illness I blame,
It seems it is laughing – and playing a game?
A game with my mind – which I have to win,
It will not win – I shall not give in.

The lord is my saviour, he
hears my call,
He send down a signal — I
do now crawl?
My prayer is answered, a
holy blessing,
Banish the devil — I hear
him hissing!

My fight is a victory, thanks
to the lord,
He helped me a lot — I had
him on board!
The scent of the devil — is
now no more
Victory is mine — I do adore.

My haunted mind is now so
blessed,
Never again will I be second
best!
The peace of my mind — is a
gift I will love,
A gift from god — as from high
above.

Victory I feel is good to me,
And the love and the honour,
is plain to see?
The trembling beat of my mind
was blind,
As now I don't fear — my haunted
mind.

SANTA GOES TO THE PHILIPPINES

Santa Claus flies through
the air towards his
destination,
Whizzing through the sky,
he's exciting all the
children.

His sleigh is packed with
presents – and Rudolph
leads the way,
And Santa never cracks
his whip – which causes
mass dismay.

Their destination is now
in sight – and Santa says;
'what a delight?'
He tells his reindeer to
now slow down – and
with land in view – it's
a fabulous sight.

With a smile on his face –
he looks around – and
he thinks; 'what a place?'
He has reached a friendly
island – an island of sheer
grace.

They see the clear blue
sea, and the tropical lush
green hills,
He says to Rudolph; 'go
and get the sacks – we'll

give the children some thrills?'
So with presents stacked
up high – Santa sets off on
his round,
Delivering all them
presents – and all without
a sound!

He can't believe the beauty,
of these islands he sees now,
Rudolph says; 'they are the
Philippines – and Santa, so
does bow.'

Santa looks amazed – and
he loves what he sees,
The beautiful Philippines –
and a crystal blue sea – and
endless rows of Christmas
trees.

This is just like my home –
it is so very beautiful,
Happiness and love are all
here – so very plentiful.

Now Santa whizzes round
the land – and he's dropping
the presents everywhere,
Then he sees a little old
lady, she's sitting in a chair?

He asks her 'how she is,
and would she like a gift?'
Then to her delight and
amazement – her grandchild,

she does lift.

Santa carries on – and goes
to every tent,
Giving gifts and smiles, and
giving lots of hugs to the
people who it's meant.

Their lives have now been
changed – thanks to Santa,
and his sleigh,
They once lived in dismay –
but happiness, now leads
the way.

His mission is now complete –
and he holds his fat old
tummy,
Wedging himself into his
sleigh, he's ready for his final
journey.

With all the friendly people
there – they wave their last
goodbye's –
And Santa waves back, and
gives a wink – as he flies off
through the skies.

The sleigh shoots away, and
Santa shouts; 'Ho, Ho, Ho,'
The people shout: 'Santa really
does exist' – as the Philippine
people now know.

Merry Christmas Santa shouts
from high up in the sky,

He loves the beautiful
Philippines – this he can't deny.

I'll see you all next year – and
that is a promise I'll keep,
As all the people in the
Philippines – drifted off into
a peaceful deep sleep.

Santa arrives home – and is
greeted by Mrs Claus,
"How was your night, my
dear, as she pats Rudolph's
shiny red nose?"

I've been to a magical land –
and I've seen it in my dreams –
And now I've actually been
there – Merry Christmas to
the Philippines.

PEACE FOR SYRIA

The world is watching –
that we know,
All the pain is felt, and
more.
The pain of the children –
and adults too,
It really does touch us,
we're the few.

They say they have a
weapon, of real harm,
And what we want –
is for them to disarm!
Not to quarrel – not to
fight,
Just sit round a table –
and talk of, what might?

The diplomacy of the
western world,
We should praise – as
we all should.
Chemical weapons have
not been found,
We want the truth –
then all will be sound!

World leaders are getting
together,
The more they talk – it
has to endeavour!
Peace will come in the
end, it will,

Then the world – will
praise, and, oh, what a
thrill?

They say there are horrors
of chemical weapons –
But there's no evidence –
as it happens!
Why do we judge? Why
do we condemn?
Why are we policing the
world, we are in?

The lives are wiped-out,
and humanity scrambles,
This all crisis is a shambles!
We can help – but in a
way, helping we can do –
As the world watches, the
talk comes through!

We should NOT go to war,
we should stay away,
But we can still help – in
a good way?
We must sit down – and
discuss this proper,
Perhaps we should recruit,
Darryl Ashton, our saviour?

We could use the poems he
writes so well,
They'll make the people of
Syria, feel so swell!
Lets try something different,
it just might work,
A poet we need – some joy

to spark!

Good luck to Syria, I mean
that so much,
We then can be friends –
and gently touch!
The touch of peace – will
finally prevail –
And that, my friends – we
all must hail!

To the world leaders – I ask
you this:
"Please don't fight – it won't
be bliss?
Let us shake hands – and all
be friends –
Believe me, I know – and
love life to the ends.

To end this conflict – is our
mission,
I start the peace – by tuning
the ignition!
We all should live as one and
all,
And life, my friends, shall be
a ball!"

It isn't hard to discuss this
now,
And if all goes well – we can
all take a bow!
Just pray a little prayer –
that's all it will take,
And peace and love – will

reign – and the hands of
power will all gladly shake!

We don't need anymore
wars – as peace is now
here,
When this does end – we
may all shed a tear?
So, to Obama, Cameron,
and Putin, and co,
Lets end this conflict now –
and forever more.

THE AUTOMATED UTILITIES HASSLE

I waited in all morning
But the gas man never came,
I had what they call a time – slot
But I didn't have a name.

So I couldn't ring his mobile
But only sit and fume,
His computer wasn't told of
The appointment, I assume.

Why is it such a hassle?
Why does no one seem to care?
About getting simple jobs done
Without tearing out my hair.

When I ring to rearrange things,
I get music or machine,
Which gives me umpteen options
But won't tell me what they mean.
get option one to five.

It's just the same with banking
If my new cheques don't arrive,
And I ring up to enquire
I get option one to five.

To speak to someone human
I must wait forever more,
Or, "Try again, please later"
What a monumental bore.

It's different if I owe them
Even quite a trivial sum,

I get a nasty letter
And the bailiffs set to come.

It's scary – most for pensioners –
How modern business works?
Run by a bunch of bullies
Or a set of useless jerks.

Why can't firms just get the message?
That we customers are sick
Of being treated as a milch cow
And addressed as if we're thick.

We have rights and we have feelings,
But it doesn't seem that way.
All we get is blasted options
And a whopping bill to pay.

Some firms are really helpful
Still a few like that remain,
And if I find a good one
I go back to them again.

If they're staffed by human beings
And treat clients with respect,
Then they're giving me – and others
The top service we expect.

Though machines have many uses
They're impersonal and slow,
And incapable of telling me
The things I need to know.

Some high – tech stuff is essential
But if I had a choice,
I'd rather tell my problem to
A living human voice.

THE AUTOMATED PHONE – IN HASSLE

Today I tried to make a call,
Insurance query, that was all.
I'd hoped to talk to someone live
Who answered queries, nine–to–
five.

Instead came a recorded voice
That told me I must make a
choice.
The voice explained that they
could clearly
Process my own type of query.

If I would hear the options given
And choose a number one to seven,
Then "press" the one that's right
for me
And I'd be answered instantly.

I listened hard to all the list
But lots of what was said I missed.
So though it taxed my ageing brain
I listened to the list again.

At first I thought that option three
Was probably the one for me'
But then it seemed that option four
Might suit my query even more.

I made my choice with breath abated,
Pressed on option four and waited,
Hoping, as I'd made a start,
It meant I would get the right
department.

I listened then to various rings,
The buzzings, clicks and tones and things.
Which made me think in sudden dread,
That they might cut me off instead.

At last, I heard a constant ring,
Which obviously I hoped would bring
A human person who was free
To talk about my policy.

The ringing stopped, I heard a click,
I got my question ready quick.
A voice came on! But oh, the pain,
A flippin' record once again!

The voice said they would take my question,
Once the lines had less congestion.
Which, of course, I swiftly knew,
Meant I was in a bloody queue.

Soon I thought I'd turn to violence
When I got some dreadful silence,
But at last a sound came through…
Recorded music! Dead on cue!

A voice kept cutting in to say
They're sorry for the long delay.
But finally a real girl came
To ask me would I give my name.

Then came' the pause, computer checks!
I guessed what she would ask me

next,
And sure enough, she made the plea –
They'd have to check security!

I answered questions one by one,
My date of birth, and then my mum,
I said her maiden name was Wyatt,
But then! Oh no! The phone went quiet!

Someone somewhere had forgotten…
Pulled a plug or pressed a button.
All my waiting on the line
Had been a total waste of time.

There was no way I'd try again,
I really couldn't stand the strain!
I've found another way that's better,
Just buy a stamp and send a letter!

FREAKY AND WACKY

The lecturer from Planet Rum
Addressed his doubtful class:
'I have some most exciting plans
Which soon will come to pass.

'We're going to visit Planet Earth
Where Earthlings all reside,
'My spaceship's at the ready,
We have to go outside.'

'But Sir,' Said little Freaky,
'Are you sure we ought to go.
'And visit those odd Earthlings
For they look bizarre, you know.'

'Yes,' said Wacky, I have heard,
They only have one head,
'And two arms, not 11,
And their eyes aren't black and red.'

'Tut, tut,' said their professor,
'I know that they look weird,
'But despite their strange appearance,
There is nothing to be feared.

'They do not like each other much
And they quarrel, fight and curse,
'Instead of finding out about
The wondrous universe

'I do not think they'll notice us,
For all the time they plan
To try to blow each other up,

Man's enemy is Man.

'Their planet, though, is beautiful,
Much better than this place.
'We need to go and live there
And supplant the human race.

'For in their self – destruction
They've lost sight of what it's worth,
'And when they blow each other up
They might blow up the Earth.'

The professor surveyed his lovely class,
So many – limbed and green,
'We'll be an asset to the Earth,
Add lustre to the scene.

'So come aboard, my beauties,
There's no better time than this,
'We'll rid the Earth of those aliens
And live a life of bliss.'

AND MOSES SAID TO THE LORD…"TEN WHAT?"

God: "What are you doing with the tablets of stone with my Ten Commandments? I thought I told you to take it down the mountain to read to the multitude".

MOSES: "Yes, you did, God, but I need to talk to you about that".

GOD: "What's to talk about. It was a simple enough task".

MOSES: "That's what I thought, until, the Health and Safety spotted me trying to carry the tablets".

GOD: "What have they got to do with it?"

MOSES: "Well, God, they reckoned that it was either going to do my back in, or I might drop it on my foot, or somebody else's foot. Anyway, H & S weren't having it. I had to fill in a risk assessment form first".

GOD: "Anything else?"

MOSES: "As a matter of fact, there is. It was then that the PC Brigade got involved. Said the title was too abrupt. Didn't leave any room for negotiation"

GOD: "That was the idea. They are my commands, that is why they are called commandments. The title stays".

MOSES: "Right, God, but there was a couple of other things they weren't happy about".

GOD: "What else were they moaning about?"

MOSES: "Well they didn't care for that bit about not worshipping any other Gods. Said it was discriminatory and might upset other religions".

GOD: "Anything else?"

MOSES: "That bit about honouring thy mother and father. They reckon in single – parent families some of the kids don't know who their father is. Sometimes the mother hasn't got a clue!"

GOD: "Go on, let's have it all".

MOSES: "The people and the politicians are dead against the word 'lie'- they say it is too judgmental. They prefer the phrase such as 'putting a spin on it' or 'presenting it in a better light' or 'in the public interest'.

GOD: "They are still liars, though".

MOSES: "Oh yes, God, they lie for a living".

GOD: "Are there any of MY commandments these various meddlers are happy about?"

MOSES: "Well, God, they're OK with 'thou shalt not kill'. And the one about stealing, although the politicians rob the people blind, but as they call it taxing apparently, it's all right"
Of course, the big stores don't agree with keeping the Sabbath special."

GOD: "I've got a good mind to send a plague of frogs to teach these sinners a lesson".

MOSES: "No God, don't do that – or we'll have the animal

rights crowd all over us like a rash!"

A BRAND NEW TOMORROW

The moon shines down,

and, oh, what a sight.

My spirit is lifted - and

feels such delight.

My hands do tremble,

it isn't good,

But my soul is troubled -

I hide under my hood.

The journey I take will

soon be over,

My brain is hurt - why

do I bother?

The life I lead is not

for me,

I look out yonder - to

the inviting sea.

I feel nothing - no love,

no life,

How I wish I had a wife.

I'd cherish and love her -

that's for sure,

Because true love my

friends, is the perfect

cure.

I stand alone against the

wall,

Hoping and praying I do

so fall.

My mind is troubled - I

feel no life,

How do I go on - I feel

such strife.

I try to grasp the air

around me,

But all I feel is more

anguish and no loyalty.

How do I manage - is

is my life?

As all I want is a loving

wife.

But my feelings are all

damaged - I do not lie,

'I can't go on - why do

I try?'

The prosecution of this

body of mine is decay,

Will it give way, and

and will happiness save

the day?

        Oh Lord, my God, please

hear my prayer -

Please send an angel to

help me to care.

Touched by an angel - is

there some magic?

'Or, will my life be oh, so

tragic?'

The scent I smell is a

holy smell,

Do I feel God - and his

love to dwell?

My soul is now blessed,

as I sleep for now,

And in dreams I go -

my soul - I shall bow.

'Thy miracle of life, is

some for me?'

A kiss from God - and

it's free.

I will be positive - that

is my aim,

To seek out a new life,

and feel no more shame.

My soul feels love - I now

thank the lord,

He answered my prayer -

he said: 'Come on board!'

'Now I'm 'FREE' - no more

sorrow,

My new life starts here -

and a brand new tomorrow.'

(There now follows a tribute poem to the brilliant football website of O-Posts – which is edited by the owner; Omar Almasri – my football poems are also on proud display on this brilliant football website. And the following poem is a special tribute to the owner, Omar Almasri and O-Posts. Enjoy the poem.)

A VERY HAPPY NEW YEAR 2017 FROM THE O-POSTS BRILLIANT FOOTBALLING WEBSITE...AND OMAR ALMASRI

A very Happy New Year
to the O-Posts football
website,
Edited by Omar Almasri -
it's a footballing delight.
See all the postings about
football as you explore,
But once you have a look -
you'll certainly want some
more.

Everything you need is
there - to brighten up
your day.
And you'll meet the
friendly editor - Omar
Almasri.
You could even contribute,
and write a blog about
football,
Go ahead, and try it - you
know you'll have a ball!

There's poems galore
about football - and so
very entertaining.
Why not take a tour - if
you get my meaning?
It is a fabulous website
and we all can take part,

Just contact Omar Almasri -
he'll welcome you with
open heart.

Happy New Year is
what I say, and welcome to 2017.
Come and join the O-Posts
team - it is the place to
be seen.
There is always plenty
to see and read - on
the O-Posts, so, behold!
Please take a seat and
rest a while - and watch
everything unfold!

And if you're a fan of
poetry - well you're in
for a treat.
Feast your eyes on this
website - for good poems,
it does create.
All the best to you all -
and a very Happy New
Year;
Just visit the O-Posts
football website - and
give an almighty cheer!!!!

BY
DARRYL ASHTON

Unsung Hero Awards 2011

Awarded to

Mr Darryl Ashton,
Blackpool

on behalf of Lancashire County Council in recognition of their exceptional volunteering work and contribution to the local community.

County Councillor Chris Hollern

Lancashire
County
Council

14 Wyndham Gardens
Blackpool
Lancashire

18th June 2009

Dear Darryl,

Thank you for your letters regarding when your poem will be read out on our show.

Apologies for the delay in getting back to you but the reason for this is that the show (which has already been recorded) will transmit the first week we are back after the summer break.

Channel 4 schedulers have not confirmed when this will be as yet. We have been told it's likely to be w/c 24th August but could be a week later.

Anyway, the show in which Jeff reads out your poem in his introduction is the Tuesday's Countdown for that week. Therefore, it will either be Tuesday 25th August or possibly Tuesday 1st September.

Sorry I can't be more specific, but watch out for the schedules nearer the time and look out for Countdown returning after the summer holidays.

Many thanks again for sending us you poem which went down really well with the studio audience.

Best wishes,

Kate

Kate Horton
Associate Producer, Countdown.

Fylde Arts Association

Fourteenth Poetry Competition

Awards and Commendations

Class A - Poem in Traditional Form — Page

First	Acaci	Elle-Marie Hinchcliffe	1
Second	My Chirpy Mate	Darryl Ashton	2
Third	Memories of Bygone Times	Darryl Ashton	3

Commended

Your Flag and your Country	Darryl Ashton	4
The Little Fir Tree	Darryl Ashton	5

Class B - Poem in Free Verse

First	Plumage	Elle-Marie Hinchcliffe	6
Second	Change of Place	Elle-Marie Hinchcliffe	7
Third	Desires	Mary Hodges	8

Commended

Sleeping Man	Anne Lockhart	9
Writing Letters	Elle-Marie Hinchcliffe	10
Silent Bird	Marjorie Nye	11
Secluded	Marjorie Nye	12

Class C - Light Verse

First	The Star-Trekking Shooting Star	Darryl Ashton	13
Second	Sleeping Partner	Mary Hodges	14
Third	A Christmas Wish	Darryl Ashton	15

Commended

Florrie	Darryl Ashton	16
Teenage Lament	Elsa Knight	18

Rose Bowls — Elle-Marie Hinchcliffe was chosen to hold the Rosie O'Callaghan Memorial Rose Bowl until the next competition.

Darryl Ashton was chosen to hold the Marjorie Pennington Rose Bowl until the next competition.

Galloway's
Society for the Blind

91 Balmoral Road
Morecambe
LA3 1SS
Tel: (01524) 414846
Fax: (01524) 414846

Dear Darryl,

Thank you so much for sending us your lovely poems and the accompanying letter.

The second package arrived safely yesterday. Everyone here has really enjoyed listening to your poems.

The Tuesday group were all very impressed by your work when they came in this week. We played your CD and everyone really enjoyed it.

We would very much like you to come along to one of our Tuesday meetings if you would like to.

I am away on holiday from 8th-15th February. I will 'phone you on my return and hopefully we can organise something.

About the website - the person responsible for putting items on our website is based in our head office in Penwortham, so, with your permission, I will forward some poems to him.

Keep up the brilliant work!

Thanks once again,

Jean D. Cavaliere

Jean D. Cavaliere

---

nalsvi — Supporting visually impaired people
website: www.galloways.org.uk
Charity No. 526088

Made in the USA
Charleston, SC
21 January 2017